Praise for *Organize Tomorrow Today*

"*Organize Tomorrow Today* helped me increase my business over 30 percent in six months and, most importantly, improved my balance at home. Small disciplines practiced every day equal success! It's a must-read for high achievers."
  —Vickie Wicks, General Partner, Edward Jones

"Dr. Jason Selk and Tom Bartow are experts at peak performance and productivity. In this book they not only teach you what to do, they teach you how to think. And that may be the difference between just knowing and succeeding."
  —Shep Hyken, *New York Times* bestselling business author of *The Amazement Revolution*

"An outstanding read. I only wish it had been around earlier in my career."
  —Dave Short, former Chairman and CEO of American Funds

"The concepts in *Organize Tomorrow Today* can be used on the playing field and in the boardroom. Jason and Tom nail it by showing all of us that self-improvement is a process and not an event. I've known both of these individuals for some time now and they both walk the walk."
  —Tom Erickson, Partner, KPMG

"The Bible says, 'As iron sharpens iron, so one man sharpens another.' Tom Bartow, through his [work] with Jason Selk [in] *Organize Tomorrow Today*, continues to sharpen me."

> —David L. Steward, Founder and Chairman of World
> Wide Technology and Founding Director of Biblical
> Business Training (BBT)

"I thoroughly enjoyed *Organize Tomorrow Today*. In particular, I embrace the simplicity of the methodology and the focus it brings to one's day."

> —David Jaeger, Treasurer, Boeing (retired)

"Selk and Bartow teach you how to develop the mental toughness needed to thrive on adversity."

> —Bobby Gassoff, Lieutenant Commander, Navy SEAL

"Whether you are currently in business or retired from the business world, as I am, the principles in *Organize Tomorrow Today* apply. If you are just entering business, this is a must-read!"

> —Pete Smith, CFO, Occidental Petroleum (retired)

"Positive, upbeat . . . actionable, attainable . . . entertaining and readable. . . . Put into practice, the skills outlined in this book can be life-changing and get you to the level of performance you crave."

> —*San Francisco Book Review*

"[*Organize Tomorrow Today*] outlines eight steps to become better organized and maximize your time. Plus, they give tips to train yourself to be more confident, energetic, and focused."

> —Kim Komando, *USA Today*

Organize Your Team Today

ALSO BY DR. JASON SELK

*Organize Tomorrow Today: 8 Ways to Retrain Your
Mind to Optimize Performance at Work and in Life*
(coauthored with Tom Bartow, with Matthew Rudy)

*10-Minute Toughness: The Mental-Training Program
for Winning Before the Game Begins*

*Executive Toughness: The Mental-Training Program
to Increase Your Leadership Performance*

Organize
Your Team
T⊘DAY

The Mental Toughness Needed
to Lead Highly Successful Teams

Dr. Jason Selk + Tom Bartow
with Matthew Rudy

Da Capo
∞
LIFE
LONG

Da Capo Lifelong Books
Hachette Book Group
1290 Avenue of the Americas, New York, NY 10104
dacapopress.com
@DaCapoPress

Printed in the United States of America
First Edition: March 2018

Published by Da Capo Lifelong Books, an imprint of Perseus Books, LLC, a subsidiary of Hachette Book Group, Inc. The Da Capo Lifelong Books name and logo is a trademark of the Hachette Book Group.

The Hachette Speakers Bureau provides a wide range of authors for speaking events. To find out more, go to www.hachettespeakersbureau.com or call (866) 376-6591.

Print book interior design by Trish Wilkinson

Library of Congress Cataloging-in-Publication Data
Names: Selk, Jason, author. | Bartow, Tom, author.
Title: Organize your team today : the mental toughness needed to lead highly
    successful teams / by Dr. Jason Selk and Tom Bartow with Matthew Rudy.
Description: First edition. | New York, NY : Da Capo Lifelong Books, [2018] |
    Includes bibliographical references.
Identifiers: LCCN 2017040202| ISBN 9780738233796 (hardcover) | ISBN
    9780738233970 (ebook)
Subjects: LCSH: Teams in the workplace—Management. | Organizational
    behavior. | Success in business.
Classification: LCC HD66 .S455 2018 | DDC 658.4/022—dc23
LC record available at https://lccn.loc.gov/2017040202

ISBNs: 978-0-73823-379-6 (hardcover); 978-0-7382-3397-0 (ebook); 978-0-7382-8476-7 (international edition)

10 9 8 7 6 5 4 3 2 1

Contents

Never criticize, nag, or razz a teammate.

—JOHN R. WOODEN

Introduction

WHAT MAKES TEAMS GREAT

You've seen the speech.

Maybe it's the World Series MVP, covered in champagne, talking about the dramatic victory his team just earned. Or it could be a CEO at an annual shareholders' meeting, talking about how proud she is that the organization crushed its financial goals.

"It couldn't have happened without the great team I have around me," the players and the CEOs usually say.

Those words come so often because they're anchored in the truth. Teams *are* a fundamental part of sports and business. Teams can only survive and thrive if they have the right composition, the right leadership, and the right metrics by which they're measured. And the teams that become dynasties? They operate at an even higher level.

The million-dollar question (or billion, depending on your team) is the same whether you're a part of a 10,000-employee Fortune 500 company or a small mom-and-pop outfit.

How?

How do you bring individuals with different talents and motivations together to form a team that consistently outperforms the competition? How do you avoid all of the standard pitfalls teams face? How do you align goals, inspire productivity, and measure performance?

How do you lead a team, and not just manage it?

How do you make yourself an essential part of your new team as quickly as possible?

In *Organize Your Team Today*, we're going to show you.

WHY US?

We've been fortunate to work with some of the highest-performing organizations in the worlds of sports and business over the past thirty years. Clients ask us to help them create cultures where every contributor can get the most out of his or her skills and talents. Part of that job involves finding the right players—and part of it comes from helping teams understand how to work with the players they have.

The two of us have a combined total of almost fifty years of experience in developing and teaching the information we bring to you in this book. Jason Selk is one of the premier performance coaches in the United States, with hundreds of professional athletes and Fortune 500 executives as his clients. As the director of mental training for Major League Baseball's St. Louis Cardinals, Jason helped the team win two World Series championships, in 2006 and 2011.

Coauthor Tom Bartow left a successful career as a college basketball coach to join Edward Jones. He became a general partner in six years and then reached similar stature at the Capital Group, parent company of American Funds. He is the only person in the financial services industry to achieve this distinction. After starting his own coaching business in 2009, he has become one of the most creative and sought-after business coaches in the nation.

Together we have merged psychology with business acumen to create a simple, usable methodology for teams and individuals. Our first book, *Organize Tomorrow Today*, was recognized by 800-CEO-READ as one of the top fifteen business books for 2016.

WHY TEAMS?

If you're familiar with *Organize Tomorrow Today*, you know that the tools to take control of your life and your performance are within your grasp. If you make a series of basic, step-by-step commitments to improve incrementally, over time you can get much more out of yourself than you ever thought possible.

Of course, teams bring a different dynamic into play. You can populate a team with a collection of A-players who all have their own ideas about what "high performance," "communication," and "setting goals" mean. But if those achievers don't come together in an effective way—both through sure-handed leadership and through their own willingness to learn how to adapt and respond to change—the team fails.

Instead of gaining exponential growth by combining the talents of different players, you get something *less* than the sum of the assembled parts.

When that happens in sports, you often hear whispers about "bad chemistry," or how the manager or coach "lost the locker room." In business, you'll hear about it when the board announces they're replacing the CEO and undertaking a reorganization. All that time, effort, and expertise that went into putting talented people in position to win under the old strategy?

Tossed.

Yet you don't have to look very far to find sports and business teams that create those dynasties. They consistently produce *more* than the sum of their parts. Team members come and go, but the framework and culture of the team stay in place, and they continue to produce championship results.

Coach John Wooden's UCLA Bruins won ten national championships in a twelve-year stretch with a variety of different players. Bill Belichick has won five Super Bowls in seventeen years with the New England Patriots—even though the NFL salary cap is designed to make it hard to keep teams together for more than a few years, and despite losing an almost constant stream of assistants and front-office executives to other teams. In business, Apple lost its founder and inspirational leader, Steve Jobs, to an extended leave for cancer treatment in 2009 and reported its best-ever quarter. When Jobs passed away in 2011, the company was prepared to move forward with Tim Cook, and has since reinforced its position as the strongest international brand in the world. In 2016, it generated almost $250 billion in revenue.

A basketball team from fifty years ago might not seem like it has a lot in common with a global tech giant, but the philosophies and strategies for team building and optimization they use are strikingly similar.

Don't just take our word for it.

Andy Hill played for three of Coach Wooden's national championship teams in the early 1970s, a time when some of the greatest players in basketball history, such as Bill Walton and Jamaal Wilkes, were also Bruins; he was a freshman when the legendary Kareem Abdul-Jabbar was a senior. After graduating from UCLA, Andy entered the television business, eventually becoming the head of CBS Productions—the team that introduced shows like *Touched by an Angel*; *Dr. Quinn, Medicine Woman*; and *Walker, Texas Ranger* to the viewing public. Later, he would reconnect with Coach Wooden to write the best seller *Be Quick— But Don't Hurry: Finding Success in the Teachings of a Lifetime.*

Andy was a part of a bona fide dynasty at UCLA, then created his own at CBS. His insights have helped Jason and Tom develop the team-based programming they use when they work with corporate clients. They have all been friends for years.

The words Andy uses to describe his time with Coach Wooden will sound very familiar as you work your way through the nine concepts we introduce in *Organize Your Team Today*:

1. Respecting Channel Capacity
2. Managing Expectations
3. Self-Evaluation
4. Turning Chemistry into Cohesion
5. Disagreeing Without Being Disagreeable
6. The No-Victim Mentality
7. Talent Selection and Development
8. The Attack Mentality
9. Making Adjustments

The essence of Andy Hill's takeaway from his decades of experience both with Coach Wooden and using the Coach's principles in his own business? Getting better is hard, and it takes work. And sometimes that work doesn't feel good. But if you focus on what you can control, select the right talent for the right role, keep it simple, and prepare fully and thoughtfully, you can thrive.

Straightforward concepts, but they have profound consequences in the business world.

Focusing on what you can control and keeping things simple means respecting and embracing channel capacity—the hardwired limit we all have in regard to how we can apply our attention. Dynasties in sports and business respect this dynamic more than any other single factor. They put great effort into not overloading their teams with blizzards of tasks and responsibilities.

Selecting the right talent for the role busts the "star player" fallacies that have become so imbedded in corporate culture. Peak performers are great to have, but the best teams have the ideal mix of stars, support players, and leaders. Every job gets done—not just the glamorous ones. Teams respond to leaders who set clear goals and establish the steps to achieve those goals. This kind of leadership creates a level of respect between the leader and the team—and among the team members—that is a catalyst for peak achievement.

In *Organize Your Team Today*, we'll take you into the trenches with some of the most successful leaders. We'll go beyond offering a laundry list of "best practices," showing you concrete and proven strategies for joining and building a team that you can put in place on day one—with no specialized training or lengthy run-up period. You'll be able to learn from the successes (and missteps) of those who have come before—and avoid the most common team traps—whether you're a relative newcomer who is joining a team or a leader looking to drive peak performance.

When Andy was installed at the helm of CBS Productions, he spent his first year getting his management team in place. In hindsight, he says, he could have moved faster, but didn't because some of the changes he had to make involved removing contributors he personally liked but weren't a good fit for the reconfigured team. A limited budget stopped him from hiring the most prominent writers. He could have used this as an excuse, and he and his team could have become victims of circumstance. Instead, Andy focused on developing the writers he had, and in doing so, he led them to higher levels of performance.

Andy built a dynasty at CBS because he figured out the metric that mattered the most—and trained his team to be relentless in attacking that metric every day. In the years before he took the role, Andy had noticed that all the television studios measured their success by the number of shows they picked up for the fall schedule. In a dramatic departure, he decided he would measure his team's success by how many pilots—or introductory episodes— he delivered that the creator of that show truly loved. It was a major adjustment from traditional "network thinking."

The reality is that most new shows fail. If a show makes it onto the schedule and sticks into its second and third and fourth seasons (and so on), that's when everybody starts to make serious money. Andy's goal was to increase the odds of getting his shows to stick on the schedule—by focusing on compelling, high-quality shows—even if that meant pitching a smaller roster of shows each fall.

As we said in *Organize Tomorrow Today*, we're not offering some kind of magic bullet that takes the work out of high-level success. We have called that book an "Owner's Manual for Doers," and that's really appropriate here, too. If you have an important goal to achieve or problem to solve, knowing what steps to take and what mistakes to avoid can give you clarity and make you more likely to succeed—but you still have to pound the nails and put in the sweat.

To some people, the idea that there isn't a hack or a shortcut might be discouraging. If that's you, you can put this book down right now. But if you're like most people we see week to week in our visits around the country, you're excited by the idea that there are guideposts left by the people and the teams who came before you. And you know how great it feels to combine hard work with good guidance and produce great results.

The book is divided into three parts:

- Consistent Winning—Chapters 1, 2, 3
- Playoff Level—Chapters 4, 5, 6
- Dynasty Level: Rarefied Air—Chapters 7, 8, 9

All the tools work together as a performance improvement plan for both work and life—but you don't even have to master them all to get a benefit. In fact, Jason and Tom don't want you to tackle them all.

Channel capacity is the key. One of the biggest mistakes people make in business and in life is that that they try to change too many things too quickly. You see it on New Year's Day, when so many people resolve to change everything they eat and go to the gym five times a week. After a burst of early enthusiasm for the new goals, reality sets in, and it gets harder and harder to cope with all the wrenching changes. At that point, it takes only a few days of "failure" to get discouraged and ditch the whole plan.

Instead, as you read this book, think about which of the nine concepts address some of the issues you're having in your professional or personal life. If you are the leader or a member of a team, think especially about the issues the team is having. Pick the *one* that resonates the most. Start with that, and commit to following the step-by-step guidelines. The key to high-level success is to pick one thing to change—yes, just one—and master it. If all you take from this book is a single, concrete change from one of the nine concepts, it's enough for you to make a true breakthrough to the next level of success—however you define it. Over time, you can build on them, one concept at a time.

Let's get on the path.

Part I

Consistent Winning

Speed the process to consistent winning by executing Chapters 1, 2, and 3. Being a consistent winner doesn't just happen; it is planned and developed.

Chapter 1

CHANNEL CAPACITY:
WHY LESS IS MORE

Channel Capacity: The limited biological bandwidth
of the human brain

More.
Faster.
Better.
Cheaper.

The chase for numbers, productivity, achievement, and results is relentless. It doesn't matter what kind of organization you're a part of. It could be a financial advisory firm, an NFL team, or a commercial real estate company. Organizations have goals, and the people in those organizations—from the leaders to those on the front lines—are held accountable if those goals aren't met.

You don't have to go very far to see examples of this out in the world. A large retailer announces huge losses and closes a bunch of its stores. An NFL team loses six games in a row and fires its entire coaching staff. A software company announces that it needs to "rightsize" and reorganize so it can more effectively compete in the marketplace.

And yet every one of those organizations had access to the very best in modern analytical data, had leadership teams made up of smart people from the best schools and with the best resumes, and had the ability to devote as much of the organization's worker horsepower to their problems as necessary.

But it didn't work.

Why?

Because the desire to do more, achieve more, and earn more has driven many modern organizations into a powerful trap that is very hard to escape. They see the ambitious goals ahead of them, and they see all of the cutting-edge information and tools available, and they turn the dial up as far as it will go. More research. More information. More people involved in the decisions. It's like walking into quicksand. Your instinct is to struggle harder and harder to kick yourself free, but the effort just sinks you deeper.

These strategies violate what we consider one of the foundations of effective performance. They violate *channel capacity*—the mental bandwidth limit every one of us has hardwired into our heads. There's a limit to what any person—or any team—can effectively manage without becoming distracted and less effective.

And when you reach that saturation point, you become far *less* effective than you would have been if you had just concentrated on one or two simple basics. When does more become less? Keep reading.

YOU MADE ME MAD

Tom had finished up a summer meeting for Edward Jones in the Colorado mountains and was waiting for his ride to the airport when one of the advisors who had been in the audience for his presentation approached him.

"Can I ask you a question? My business has hit a wall. . . . I'm having big-time problems increasing my production, and I've tried everything," the man said. "I need some help."

Tom responded with a quick, simple question.

"Today is Friday. You got here yesterday. How many days this week did you get out of the office and go see people?"

The man went quiet for what turned into an awkward length of time before answering.

"Well, I was really busy getting ready to come to this meeting," he said. "It was a short week, so I wasn't able to get out."

Tom responded with another simple question.

"How badly do you want to get to the next level? If you do, then get out of the office and go see seven people every day. No matter what, get that one thing done."

It looked like the man was expecting something more substantial, and he shrugged his shoulders and thanked Tom for his time.

Six months later, Tom returned to Colorado to meet with some of the advisors who were relatively new to the business— including the man who had asked for the extra help.

The meetings were scheduled to start at 8:30 a.m., but thirty minutes early, the man from the previous meeting walked up to Tom.

"Do you remember me?"

Before Tom could answer, the man continued.

"I'm not coming to your meeting today," he said. "You know why? You made me mad! I was asking for your help, and you gave me what I thought was blow-off advice. I decided I was going to do what you said, so that when you came back I could show you why you were wrong—why your advice wasn't going to help."

Tom waited for the punch line.

"So I did what you said. I got out of my office and saw seven people every day. It was the only thing I did differently, and the only goal I gave myself. And it worked. This meeting is only for people at my original level. I've gone up two levels since then. I just wanted to come and say thanks, and I'm out of here!"

Channel capacity isn't some clever management consulting catchphrase we've invented to spice up our speeches. It comes from science. **People can consistently hold only three things in "working memory" at one time.** Think of it as juggling. You can handle three balls in the air, but if another ball gets thrown into the mix, you're likely to drop all of them. And that's with things that are already understood. **When it comes to learning new things, channel capacity is one thing at a time.**

Think of your brain as being like the photo album on your phone. Once the capacity for memory is reached, there is no room for new photos. To free up space, you have to delete some pictures before you add new ones, and modern technology helps you make those choices. Unfortunately, with your brain, when new information goes in, current information is being randomly erased. If that happened with your phone, just think how careful you would be with your photo taking.

As we explained in our first book, *Organize Tomorrow Today*, with our multiple screens, super-powerful smartphones, and constant multitasking—we have pushed ourselves to the point of massive oversaturation.

This happens through a series of seemingly logical steps.

1. A leader intuitively understands that a goal is too ambitious to be achieved, so he or she tries to utilize every tool and technique for increasing production. But when individuals begin to struggle or fall behind, the leader fails to honor channel capacity. Instead of creating a more specific focus on only the most important activities to drive results, more ideas and suggestions are piled on.
2. The leader knows that good information is good. More good information must be better—or so the information

myth goes—so he or she feeds it to the team with a fire hose to try to help it solve the problem and achieve the goal.

3. If the team does come up with a solution that is "simple," the leader thinks there must be a flaw in the process—because "complex" means "sophisticated" and "simple" means "unsophisticated." Just because we live in a complicated world with big problems doesn't mean that the solutions to some of those problems aren't simple.

We see this every single day when we travel the country to talk to different organizations about their performance process. **Many people are asking too much of their minds to perform at their peak on their most important tasks.** It might sound counterintuitive, but it's true: highly successful people never get everything done in any one given day, but they always get their most important things done each and every day.

Running your mental machinery at more than its capacity can work for short bursts of time, but when you make it a habit, over the long term you have the same issues you would with an engine—things begin to break down. Both individuals and teams can burn out and stagnate. Execution becomes inconsistent, new team members struggle to integrate themselves into the group, and teamwork bogs down.

Despite everyone's high hopes, the team fails.

It's an epidemic in the business world. But unlike some epidemics, for this one there's a cure.

Our goal here is to get you and your team focusing laser-like on the most important information and activities—and *only* that information and those activities. That is where efficiency and effectiveness can be found.

HONORING CHANNEL CAPACITY

When teams become dysfunctional, they're usually very ready to listen to us when we come for a consultation. But the much more dangerous problem comes with teams that are already "winning"—however the organization defines it.

They're working well together, making more sales, earning more money, and the inevitable conversation starts. How do we squeeze more out of the team? How do we produce more? They're doing great, so why not move over some of the projects from the teams that aren't doing too well?

The intentions are fine, but by overwhelming channel capacity, managers and leaders aren't getting the increased production and profit they expect. They're actually creating a team that performs *worse* than before—and gets less done, less efficiently.

We're not talking about making normal productivity demands from a team within its same sphere of responsibility. If you're coaching a football team and your offensive tackles have two main jobs they're responsible for, you can demand increased performance in those metrics. But if you decide to get your offensive tackles to be really great special teams players just in case they're needed—and move them to those practices for a couple hours per week—you're endangering their productivity at their main job.

If you have a team of salespeople who are killing it getting your new software packages out into the marketplace, you're playing with fire if you decide to cross-train them on the extended service package you also offer because the team you have in place on that line isn't doing what you expect. By increasing the various demands on a team's attention, you're limiting its productivity in the job it does very well, only to get what might not be any real improvement in the other task. In other words, by asking them to multitask, you're probably losing all around.

We like to tell all of our clients the same thing when it comes to channel capacity. Either you honor it or you put your productivity at risk.

What do violations of channel capacity look like in the real world?

Let's start with something familiar to anybody who has ever worked in an organization.

Meetings.

If you're running meetings and there are more than three subjects to be covered, you're violating channel capacity. If you're sending people out of the meeting with more than one improvement or action being emphasized, you're violating channel capacity.

How do you avoid the temptation to pile on?

First, **reject** the idea that *your* situation and *your* team are different and somehow special. You might think that your team will be able to work harder and multitask more effectively than most others, so you don't have to pay attention to channel capacity. You might even believe that simply demanding more from your people is enough of a motivator. You would be wrong.

Remember, channel capacity is biological. Your players may have the discipline and motivation to do more for a short period of time. However, when it comes to long-term performance, **no one beats channel capacity for long**.

Next, **resist** the basic principle that more knowledge equals more productivity. We know—there's a reason people go to fancy colleges and expensive graduate schools. It's to get more knowledge. But it isn't what you know that accomplishes goals. It's what you do.

Within the dynamic of a team, you have different team members with different training and knowledge. Unless the team knows in the most basic terms what the one main thing is that needs to be accomplished, all of that knowledge and information is wasted—and most of it is used in opposition to itself.

Remember the financial advisor who asked Tom what he needed to do to increase his level? Tom had all kinds of tools at his disposal to talk about increased advisor performance. They could have discussed sales techniques, client diversification, or any of a number of techniques—all of which are important to learn. But Tom understood what the *first* problem was to be solved, and *what* was required to address that first problem. The "one thing" was seeing more clients, and the "what" or "how much" was to go see seven of them.

It wasn't magic. It was focus on the first, biggest goal.

The third piece doesn't take any special knowledge, either. It's **repeating** your best practices. Knowing what you're doing well and repeating it is good programming. The team refines its ability to execute its job, and it becomes quicker, stronger, and better at doing so. When you watch one of Nick Saban's practices at the University of Alabama, you see a marvel of efficiency and focus. Players are intensely drilled—repeatedly—on how to achieve their simple objectives on the football field. The repetition takes the thinking out of it. On game day, they know what they're supposed to do, and they go out and do it.

You might have noticed that the keywords from these three ideas go very well together—and that there are only three of them. We want them to be simple to follow and easy to remember. Because that honors channel capacity!

1. Resist—thinking you can beat channel capacity.
2. Reject—the idea that more is always better.

3. Repeat—the message of how important it is to honor channel capacity.

EDWARD JONES: THE FIRST "ONE-PERSON BRANCH OFFICE"

Most people have seen the Edward Jones name on a building or a sign or in an advertisement on television. More than 7 million people invest with the company, and it has more than $900 billion in assets under management.

But most people don't know how the company started. Edward D. Jones Sr. started a small brokerage firm in St. Louis, and his son, Ted, came to work for him after returning from the Merchant Marines after World War II. After a few years in business, Ted called on the owner of a large brick company to invest with the Jones brokerage firm—and while the man didn't end up investing with the company, he was very impressed with Ted Jones.

A few years later, when the owner of the brick company decided to have a stock offering, he met with a variety of firms around St. Louis. Edward D. Jones's company was one of the smallest to attend the meeting, but the company owner raved about his experience with Ted Jones. Mr. Jones Sr. committed to taking a large chunk of the stock offering to move to his firm's clients.

Mr. Jones Sr. came back to the office and confided in his son about one problem: he was worried he might have bitten off more than he could chew. In order to move the large quantity of stock that his father had agreed to place, Ted Jones started a branch office in the town where the brick factory was located. The idea worked, and a local banker suggested to Ted Jones that he spend his time opening branches. Ted opened another office in Pueblo, Colorado.

But in the early 1950s, there wasn't a simple way to transfer stock orders from Colorado to St. Louis. Unbeknownst to his father, Ted committed to having wire run from his new satellite office in Colorado to the office in central Missouri and on to St. Louis.

When Mr. Jones Sr. got the bill for the wire, he was enraged.

Ted's response?

"We'll just put offices all along that wire to pay for it."

The one-person brokerage office idea was born, and it was up to Ted Jones to make it work.

Brokerage firms can fail for a million different reasons, but Edward Jones grew from 35 brokers to more than 14,000 because the company followed a mandate established by Ted from the very beginning.

When he got to a new city and established an office, he hit just two main points for the new brokers there.

Brokers needed to meet with twenty people every day.

And brokers needed to open ten new accounts per month.

As the company grew, it certainly had some more complex internal strategies. But to the brokers, the message was a simple and unified one—20/10.

The message was clear and simple. It honored channel capacity, and it helped team members remain confident and diligent even in tough economic times.

GREAT LEADERS DON'T PILE ON

We can debate what particular skills great leaders have—and they have a variety of them. But one thing they have in common is that they put their people in the best position to win. Ted Jones has done it in the business world, and Bill Belichick does it better than anyone in professional football. There is a reason they call the New England Patriots the NFL's ultimate dynasty.

Hundreds of books have been written trying to decipher the alchemy of leadership greatness, but to us, it starts by creating an atmosphere that respects channel capacity. Teams perform to their fullest potential because each individual on the team is operating at a high level without feeling exhausted, overwhelmed, disrespected, resentful, or burned out. Each person knows his or her role, and no one feels pressured to solve all the problems that exist outside his or her role.

Ask any player who has spent a season with Coach Belichick, and he will tell you that the coach is not an easy man. He works his players incredibly hard, and he holds them to high standards. But Belichick's players know their roles, and Belichick understands how to push them within the parameters of channel capacity to inspire elite performance on narrow tracks. Tom Brady runs the offense like a maestro while coordinator Matt Patricia executes the defensive game plan.

In the 2017 Super Bowl, the Patriots had the most adversity a team could face. They were down 28–3, and they hadn't done anything to inspire confidence that this trend would change. But leaders and teams who respect channel capacity have a powerful weapon when they face those kinds of situations. Team members know they only have to dominate in their own roles to overcome. They simply need to be the best at doing their particular job. Brady said in his post-game interview that there was no panic in the locker room at the half. They were not overwhelmed, and the team knew what it had to do to execute its second-half plan. They wound up completing the greatest comeback in Super Bowl history, winning 34–28.

Tom Bartow had a similar experience while he was with the American Funds mutual fund group—but without the worldwide television audience (and the half-time performance by Lady Gaga). In the early 1990s, the company had decided to bring a new fund to market—something it did very rarely, and only when a fund had been thoroughly vetted. The goal was to sell $500 million of this new international fund, which would be a challenge, considering the market for that product was lukewarm, at best.

At the time, the company had four service centers across the United States—in Indianapolis; San Antonio; Hampton Roads, Virginia; and Brea, California. Each center contained a group of what are known as *internal wholesalers*—fund experts whose job it is to provide information to financial advisors so they can keep their clients informed of new products in the markets. If the internal wholesalers don't do a good job presenting a new investment to the advisors, that new product doesn't get any traction in the retail market with clients.

This fund launch would be a struggle, and the American Funds management was worried that the $500 million sales goal was too aggressive. Tom suggested a new approach—one that honored channel capacity.

The internal wholesalers would do the same thing at the same time for one hour each day of the week and present the new fund to the advisors. The logistics were certainly daunting. There were multiple wholesalers in different offices with different time zones, and they had different management styles and different skill levels. And they were presenting an investment into a market that wasn't exactly clamoring for it.

Tom's plan was to channel all of the internal wholesalers' energy into an "hour of power," as the managers called it—a concentrated effort with simple parameters, clear goals, and clear rewards.

For the same hour each day, each internal wholesaler would call as many advisors as they could. The regional site that could make the most contacts—not sales, but "contacts"—at the end of each week got a small prize, like movie tickets. All of the internal wholesalers would be rowing in the same direction, toward the same goal, at the same time.

How did it honor channel capacity? The internal wholesalers had only one deliverable. It was to make as many contacts as they could, and it was for only one hour. They knew the stakes, and they knew the rewards. The managers at each location handled the project beautifully.

The result? The total amount raised was over $700 million—making it one of the most successful fund launches in the history of the company. It didn't come from any elaborate marketing plan, an advertising program, or promotional fees sent out through the sales chain. It was a laser-like focus on the single most important action by a group of people all pulling toward the same goal.

Once you start respecting channel capacity—and tailoring your teams' responsibilities to embrace it—some amazing things start to happen. Teams begin to play to their potential—the space at the peak of their collective ability, where they're performing at a high level without feeling exhausted or burned out. They're challenged, but not overwhelmed.

Teams and their members are liberated by the idea that they're going to focus on the few important tasks. That sounds obvious and intuitive, but very few teams end up in that place. They spend most of their time and energy working on the *urgent* tasks—the ones that get most of the clamoring and chatter—not the most *important* ones.

Need an example? Let's say there's a report that leadership wants to consider at a meeting on Friday. It's Monday, and the team has to commit all of its resources to producing that report by Thursday afternoon, so it can be ready. Leadership wants it, but do they truly want it at the expense of, say, the closing of a sale with a gigantic new client? But the work of actually *doing* business will get put aside to solve an urgent task that doesn't necessarily align with the big-picture goal of the organization.

And even if your answer to that situation is to say, "Well, people will just have to stay late and get *both* the report and the big sale put together," you're missing the bigger picture. You can crank up the responsibility and pressure on the team to multitask and finish those jobs, but you're losing something at both ends. The sales process won't be handled as well as it could be, and the report will probably be sloppier than it should be.

And even if the team is able to handle the multitasking in the short term and get both done, what does that mean for the long term? The leaders of the team will get what they want, when they want it, but they will continue to pile on the responsibilities and expectations.

Then it just becomes a matter of *when* something breaks, not *if*.

"3 MOST IMPORTANT" / "1 MUST"

The human brain is like a very large sponge. Now imagine holding the sponge over a bucket full of water. If you submerge the sponge deep into the water and then lift that sponge out, what happens? Of course, water pours out of the sponge. That's exactly like what occurs when our brains overload channel capacity.

To make matters worse, as the sponge (your brain) ages, it becomes less and less able to hold water.

Generally speaking, most adults don't know how easy it is to improve their skill level. Honoring channel capacity by focusing on only one improvement at a time speeds the process. **Understanding channel capacity is the first step to controlling consistency.**

To better respect channel capacity, think about three categories where channel capacity is often not respected.

Information: On a daily basis, how much information are you taking in? If you are like most people, you are reading multiple blogs and articles, listening to a podcast or two, staying informed on current events, and keeping track of social media updates.

Remember, the more information you pour in, the more pours out. The real problem is that the information coming out is *randomly* selected. You can't control what you forget. That's bad, really bad. This is exactly why you must choose wisely what you inform yourself of.

We suggest that you choose no more than one information source daily to learn from. Don't feel like you need to spend an hour reading or learning daily to grow. Remember the sponge analogy. Instead of submerging the entire sponge, try dipping a corner into the information water. If it's done consistently, spending even five minutes per day learning reliable information is an extremely effective method of educating yourself.

Action: Remember, **highly successful people never get everything done in any given day, but they always get the most important things done each and every day**. Top producers have learned to identify and attack their three most important daily activities (otherwise known as *process goals*). The key is to know in advance what your three most important activities are before the day even begins.

If you don't know your process goals (three most important daily activities), take a moment right now and figure them out. We call these the "3 Most Important," and it's a key concept in our approach. These three things may change occasionally, but for most people—and most teams—the three most important daily activities remain the same. **It's the consistency of doing what's most important that causes greatness.**

Write your process goals down on paper and post them on your wall so that you cannot forget those key drivers. Once you know your three most important daily activities, then block time out for them daily to make sure they are completed.

Improvement: Improving is definitely important; however, be very careful about trying to improve too many things or trying to improve too much all at once. Most people don't realize that they are only one improved skill away from breaking through to the next level of success. It's very common to become motivated or inspired to change only to bite off more than what's consistently doable. Change can certainly occur with this all-too-common approach, but it's generally short-lived.

The most common issue we see with individuals we work with is that they try to make multiple improvements at once. Trying to lose twenty pounds, improve your marriage, and increase production at work at the same time is a recipe for inconsistency.

The same is true of teams. It would be very similar to asking the offensive line of your football team to master three new blocking schemes for the upcoming week's opponent. Trying to install multiple new schemes on top of the already necessary skills causes a breakdown in the mind's ability to effectively remember all the information, thus leading to poor execution.

Remember, it has almost nothing to do with how hard a person tries. It's a biological issue. When the brain becomes saturated, something must give.

When you know your three most important activities for each day, whether at the individual or the team level, figure out which one is the absolute most important one to do. We call this the "1 Must." Growth and progress become easy when you know each day, even before the day begins, the one most important activity you are going to focus on. It's important to complete your "1 Must" as early in the day as possible.

If you have not already identified your "1 Must"—as an individual, or as a team—take a moment now and do so. Chances are this will remain fairly consistent. However, if need be, spend two or three minutes on this priority-setting task each day. On a personal level, you can write them down. At the team level, you can simply remind your team members often of their "3 Most Important" tasks and their "1 Must."

DON'T "OVER-COACH"

The temptation is always there. When you have authority and unlimited information, your first instinct is often going to be to overload and over-manage, or to impose your will and your process on the team.

One of the traits that made legendary college basketball coach John Wooden so successful was that he wasn't consumed with imposing his concrete "formula" on every player. He treated his players as individuals, tailoring his approach so that he could get the most out of each individual. He didn't treat Bill Walton and Kareem Abdul-Jabbar the same, because they were different men with different personalities and different motivations. But they both became All-Americans.

If you've watched any television sports lately, you've probably seen the analysis that goes on at halftime, with the table full of talking heads analyzing every inch of what happened during the action in the first part of the game. Coach Wooden's approach is still relevant today.

When he was walking into the locker room for halftime, he only wanted to know three statistics—his team's shooting percentage, the opposing team's shooting percentage, and his team's number of turnovers, which he saw as missed opportunities.

As Coach Wooden used to tell Tom frequently, "the biggest mistake coaches make is, they over-coach." You are over-coaching if you are not respecting channel capacity. Every person should know their "3 Most Important" and their "1 Must." Coach Wooden might not have known the scientific underpinnings to his approach, but the way he did things turned out to be ideal for peak performance. Coach Wooden often said that "good things come in 3's."

As we've already stated, any individual operates at peak performance when respecting channel capacity, and that means sticking to just three separate ideas. And the same is true for a team. But when that same person or team is *learning* a new concept, the number drops down to one.

Think back to the last off-site "training session" you had. Maybe it was a three-hour session where you were supposed to learn a new software or customer resource management protocol. What happened? You were probably bombarded with a hundred rules, requirements, and strategies, and left with a giant binder of information to learn.

If that was your experience, you were set up to fail.

It happens all the time in more subtle ways, too. As the leader, you might call your team into a meeting to talk about a new initiative. You're probably excited to get started, and you want to give your team the best possible chance to do well. So you cover five things in the meeting, along with three process improvements you want to implement. You've left your team with five things to remember, and they leave the meeting wondering exactly how to prioritize all of the pieces.

We are not saying that it isn't essential over time to cover all five things. We are saying not to try to cover all five at once. Remember the rule of "3 and 1." Three items can be covered, and of the three, create a primary focus on one. Have another meeting later to cover the additional information, if need be.

You can truly separate yourself from the competition by deleting material that isn't otherwise highly relevant. **When in doubt, delete.**

Just like a football game or a basketball game, situations in business are always changing. The players on your team are always changing. But by respecting channel capacity and projecting a unified, simplified message, you're making it just as easy for the veteran members of the team to thrive as it is for new members of the team to understand how to find their place.

As the leader, you have to constantly monitor your messages to the team and make sure you're not overloading it. "When in doubt, delete," is one of our favorite sayings. If it is not critical, or absolutely necessary for success, get rid of it. Deleting information and assignments will increase your team's ability to focus and execute its most important activities. The best leaders are constantly asking themselves:

1. What is the primary goal?
2. What is the single most important task?
3. What can be deleted?

Great leaders understand that teaching their team members to respect channel capacity makes it much easier for *everybody* to have next-level success. It comes because when team members—and teams as a whole—concentrate on just the most important priorities, they get a crucial "run-over effect" that builds something no great team can work without: self-confidence.

Self-confidence is the number one variable for human performance. If self-confidence is high, individuals typically do well. When self-confidence is low, it is a bad sign for performance.

When a team focuses and successfully executes on one important task, the self-confidence of all its members increases—not just in the most important task, but across the board. The team has an increased belief in its abilities, and it relishes the next task coming to it. Its performance "magically" improves, except there's nothing magic about it.

It's science, and it's intentional.

"NAIL" THE MOST IMPORTANT

Ironically, the temptations for members of a team are similar to the ones leaders experience. If you're on the team, you're going to be tempted to try to take on more to "show your stuff," and to play the political game that is a part of so many cultures. And you're going to be tempted to arm yourself with as much information as possible to bring to the group.

But the most self-aware—and successful—team members develop an accurate self-assessment of their own channel capacity. They figure out the best way to integrate new information and the best way to focus on the most crucial task. Communicating those qualities is just as much the responsibility of the team member as recognizing and developing them is for the team leader.

Jason Selk's experience working with professional baseball players during his time with the St. Louis Cardinals proves this out. During one season, he worked extensively with two players who were both instrumental in helping the team win the 2011 World Series. But when it came to channel capacity they were very different from each other.

The first player found a lot of success when he boiled down his actionable list to one consistent focal point. He approached every time at bat the same way—"see it early, short swing." He would find the ball as early as possible coming out of the pitcher's hand, and then he would follow through with a short, compact swing. There were times when different coaches would try to get him to change his approach for different circumstances or different pitchers, but he stayed true to his own personal channel capacity, trusted his instincts, and kept it simple. He carved out a ten-year career in the major leagues, hitting nearly .300, by focusing only on that one procedure while at the plate.

The second player had a completely different style. He found that establishing a specific approach each day worked best for him. The approach he chose varied. It depended on that day's pitcher, the ballpark, and the weather conditions. On one day, his focus might be "load early, see it deep, 85 percent"; on another, it might be "look outside half, go away," or maybe even something as simple as "attack, attack, attack." Even though his focus changed, he knew what his approach was going to be before each game, and he always respected channel capacity by keeping it to no more than three focal points.

That player also had a very solid professional career, with statistics very similar to the first player's. They both honored channel capacity, but they did it in different ways. The key was that they both took the time to figure out what worked best for them within the channel capacity concept.

You don't have to be a professional baseball player to have your own turn at bat. It could be a sales call, or an assignment to produce the design for a new widget.

What will you say to yourself when you're getting ready to bat?

When you're a part of the team, your goal is to become integrated—and to become irreplaceable. There are very specific questions you can ask yourself that will make that process as clear as a floodlit runway on a clear night.

1. What is the most important task I need to master?
2. What are the two or three most important focal points for me while completing this task?
3. Who in this organization is the best at this task, and how can I learn from them?

The simple answers to questions like these—from leaders and team members—are what dynasties are made of.

TEACH IT

This is the first of nine "Teach It" sections—one for each chapter of the book. These sections take advantage of a simple concept: if you teach something that is new to you to just one other person, it will significantly increase your learning. If you are a team leader, you can teach the ideas in this book to your team members.

The first thing for you to teach someone else is the concept of channel capacity. The thing is, inevitably, people don't listen, because they think they are special enough to beat channel capacity and improve more than one thing at a time. The rule we like to follow to go with the channel capacity idea is "1 thing, 1 inch, daily." Can you imagine if you improved even just one inch a day from now until the end of next year? Where would you be if you did this for five years? Ten years? From now until the end of your life? Imagine how much better of a person we would all be if we did this.

TRUST US ON THIS . . . YOU WILL EXPERIENCE A MUCH FASTER PATH TO SUCCESS BY CHOOSING ONLY ONE THING AT A TIME TO IMPROVE.

INVERT

(By inverting any fundamental you can learn more)

If you don't learn to respect channel capacity, the members of your team will be extremely busy but not highly productive. More than likely there will be a lack of balance in people's lives and the team will be unhealthy.

"3 MOST IMPORTANT" FOR THE TEAM TO REMEMBER

1. The human brain has a limited capacity for focus and attention. The brain can manage three things at a time in working memory and can focus on just one thing at a time for making an improvement, consistently.
2. Overloading channel capacity is the main cause of inconsistency. The brain *randomly* releases information and attention to make room for the new information and attention coming in.
3. Highly successful people never get everything done in any given day, but they always get their most important things done each and every day.

"1 MUST" TAKEAWAY FOR TEAMS

Complete your "3 Most Important" / "1 Must" daily activities (process goals) as early as possible in your day.

Chapter 2

MANAGING EXPECTATIONS: TRUST OR SUSPICION

Managing Expectations: Letting people know up front the good and bad of what they should expect about being in a relationship with you

Whatever business you're in, you know "The Promise."

It'll be done by Tuesday.
I can do it for 25 percent cheaper.
This one is twice as good as the last version.
It will be no problem.

It even happens at home. You probably don't have to think back too far to remember the contractor who promised that your new bathroom would be done in three weeks—but you were still going to the gym to shower three months later. Or the dealer who swore the used car you were buying was the most reliable one he had on the lot. Even the pizza guy who promises that your order will be there in twenty minutes doesn't get it right half the time.

What do all of these situations have in common?

They're all promises people make to try to build a relationship and get approval. But what every one of these transactions does is *set expectations.* And when the person on the promise side fails to deliver, they've mismanaged those expectations—and they've made it hard for you to trust them.

It's why many people view salespeople with suspicion. It's why the sales associate at the car dealership tells you this is his or her rock-bottom price, but you don't stop negotiating. It's why your contractor quotes you a price and a finish date and you mentally add money and add days to his or her promise. And it's why we end up having to treat so many people in the business world— even people on our own teams—with suspicion instead of trust.

Why make it so hard? If you can learn how to manage expectations for yourself and those around you and deliver relentlessly on those expectations, you are setting yourself and your team up with a distinct advantage over the competition.

Predictability and follow-through build trust, and trust is the foundation of any great team.

In his great book *The Seven Habits of Highly Effective People*, author Stephen Covey said that *every* relationship breakdown is the result of expectations not being managed correctly. That book has sold almost 30 million copies, and Covey has been called one of the twenty-five most influential people in the world by *Time* magazine.[1]

But ask yourself one question: How many times have you been to a leadership conference, a 360-degree review with your supervisor, a team planning meeting, or a skill development seminar and heard somebody talk about managing expectations as a skill?

To properly manage expectations, you must let people know the good and the bad of what they should expect about being in a relationship with you. **In business, it is commonplace for expectations about time, service, and cost to go unmanaged.**

When was the last time you actually sat down and thought

about critical points in your organization's or team's decision-making processes where expectations should be managed?

We are not referring to under-promising and over-delivering here. Managing expectations means you tell people up front exactly what they should expect, and then you deliver what you said you would, and you deliver it on time. It's about being genuine and honest, and then doing whatever it takes to honor your word.

We've been traveling together for close to ten years, talking to different organizations about peak performance, and managing expectations is something that almost never comes up before we bring it up. When done properly, managing expectations can speed up the process for any team achieving success; expectations that are mismanaged are the foundation for disaster. That single factor is what Stephen Covey calls the fundamental cause of *all* relationship breakdowns.

You've seen it happen in your organization, on your teams, and in your family. When expectations don't get established and managed effectively, relationships can and do get damaged. Eventually, those relationships break. You lose a client. An employee leaves the team or leaves the organization. A marriage doesn't survive.

We've seen that this is a subject that is just not talked about enough. And judging by the results that many organizations, teams, and families see, it's a skill most people find very difficult even to improve upon, let alone master. This seems to happen for two main reasons—one that comes from the heart and one that comes from the head.

At our core, we all want to be loved and accepted. That is a basic human need. We are social beings, and we're motivated to tell people things that will increase our chance to be loved—literally and figuratively. Most people aren't evil, and they don't go out of their way to say things that aren't true. And when you're the contractor making the dollar or delivery date promise, you probably even (optimistically) think you can make it happen. But life gets in the way, and what was doable when you were making the deal isn't doable anymore.

It happens all the time in organizations across the business world. When a company goes through two or three years of strong sales and employees get fat bonuses, the smaller bonuses that come with the inevitable leaner year are often met with resentment. What the leader needed to do from the beginning was to say that bonuses will always be tied to the company's growth rate and bottom line success, and yes, there will be some down years along with those up years. It's simple to do, but it almost never happens that way. Most people don't want to be the bearer of potentially bad news.

The second reason this issue is so persistent is that most people do not think strategically enough. The best chess players are always thinking multiple moves ahead of their current move. The rest of us mortals are usually consumed with the move right in front of us. That's not a criticism. It's just reality. And when you're focused on the move in front of you, ironically, you don't often see the hole you're about to step into.

Take the wife who texts her husband to say she'll be home at 6:00 for dinner. She has a 3:30 meeting with a client that goes very well, and the client insists that they sign the paperwork and close the sale right afterward. This pushes the wife's evening well past 6:00, and she misses the dinner her husband made for her and the kids. The husband is annoyed, and the wife is resentful that the husband seems to be punishing her for her success. But the real issue doesn't have anything to do with any of that, and the whole thing could have been sidestepped if the wife had managed expectations properly, by thinking about a few of the possible outcomes instead of just the one that was most obvious. She could have said: "I'm meeting with a big client at 3:30, and I'm hoping to be done in time to be back by dinner. But if things go well it might run long. I'll text you when I'm done."

DO YOUR JOB, OR ELSE . . .

When Jason Selk was hired as the director of sport psychology for the St. Louis Cardinals in 2006, there was no ambiguity about the team's expectations. The assistant general manager, John Mozeliak (who is now the team's president of baseball operations), told Jason that if the players he was working with didn't improve more than the players he wasn't helping, he'd be fired immediately.

The Cardinals' management of expectations didn't stop with Jason. He saw from the inside how one of the strongest organizations in sports built a culture that Fortune 500 companies spend tens of millions of dollars to try (usually unsuccessfully) to emulate. Every player on the roster knew what his responsibilities were, both day to day and season to season. And those expectations were clear to everyone—no exceptions.

Knowing what was expected, Jason was determined to fit in with this focused, success-oriented culture. He resolved to be the first person to get to the spring training complex in the morning and the last person to leave at night.

The next morning, at about 5:30, Jason pulled into the dark parking lot and saw seven other cars already in the lot. As he let himself through the outside gate, he could hear something that sounded like gunshots going off every few seconds. After walking a few yards, he could see the lights on in one of the batting cages. As he got closer, he could see that it was Albert Pujols—the defending National League MVP.

Even though it was well before most of the rest of the team would arrive, Pujols was in the cage in full attack mode. There was no just going through the motions because it was early in the spring. Jason watched for a minute or two, and then Albert turned around and saw him. He gave him a cold look that clearly indicated he wasn't interested in having an audience or any distractions. He was there to work on his skills and do his job.

It was clear even that early in the season that this was a special group. To be a part of it meant that you had to live up to your end of the deal, or you weren't going to be a Cardinal. It wasn't just a "corporate credo," either. Walt Jocketty, Tony La Russa, and Dave Duncan (the general manager, manager, and pitching coach at the time) were some of the most accountable people you'll ever run into in sports or business. Pujols and Chris Carpenter were the two best players on the team, and they were also the two hardest workers. They did what they said they would do: they met and exceeded expectations daily.

That year, the team fought through plenty of adversity and injuries in the regular season, but they still managed to win their division. They were underdogs in every playoff series they were in, but they beat the San Diego Padres in the Division Series, the New York Mets in the National League Championship Series, and the Detroit Tigers in the World Series. They earned their tenth—and probably most unlikely—world championship in franchise history.

MANAGING EXPECTATIONS WITH BRICKS

Prior to becoming a financial advisor, Tom Bartow was a college basketball coach. For basketball players, the currency is "PT— Playing Time." Playing time is a cherished commodity. In recruiting potential players, it was vital to manage expectations about how much playing time a star high school player might get as a freshman.

If you over-promised on playing time and it didn't work out, the player might leave or become a detriment to your team. If you under-promised and painted a bleak picture, you might not convince the player to attend your university. It's a tenuous situation.

When Tom became a financial advisor, he recognized that talking with clients and explaining investments to them were really no different from recruiting. Over-promise, and the clients might leave; under-promise, and they might not invest.

In training, Tom had the good fortune to learn from an experienced advisor, Jim McKenzie. Jim was ranked by *Research* magazine, put out by ThinkAdvisor, as one of the top ten advisors in the country, and he was a master at managing expectations. He told clients how they should expect their investments to perform over "meaningful periods of time," and he was relentless about sharing the good and the bad of what they should expect from markets. Tom followed McKenzie's methods verbatim and it worked.

In his second year as an advisor, Tom was referred to a couple nearing retirement. Jigs and Loy Whalen represented the fabric of America; they were hardworking, family oriented, and always looking to help others. Jigs, a wiry young sixty-one-year-old, worked at the American Electric Power Plant swinging a sledgehammer for most of the day. His wife, Loy, worked at their church. They were true middle-class America. Their dream was to someday retire and be able to tour the country to visit their children and grandchildren. A camper pulled behind a pickup would serve their purposes.

The Whalens had never invested before meeting Tom. They were savers, using the bank. To invest in something that was not insured was a big step for them. Tom explained the various choices and told them about mutual funds, making sure to manage their expectations. He stated: "Here is what you should expect. . . . In

any normal four-year period, you should expect to see your investments go up three out of four years. Once out of four years you
should expect to see your investments go down in value. . . . Just
remember, three up and one down."

The Whalens chose to use conservative mutual funds for their
IRA contributions. Their attitude was, "We'll give this a try and
see what happens." One year later the Dow Jones Industrial Average was down, and so were the Whalens' IRAs. Tom scheduled
an appointment with them to discuss the results, and he hoped
they would make another IRA contribution.

In the meeting, Jigs stood up holding the IRA statements and
said to Tom, "I have been doing the numbers on our IRAs. Mine
is down over 20 percent, and Loy's is down just a little less than
mine. Why should we invest with you again?"

Before Tom could say a word, Loy interrupted, "Jigs, Tom sat
in that very chair last year and told you to expect these investments to go down once out of every four years. Write him another
check."

As Tom was driving back to his office, with the additional
checks from the Whalens for the year's IRA contribution safely
tucked away in his briefcase, he thought to himself, "I just got
lucky." Loy Whalen had remembered to expect the investments to
go down once every four years. What if she hadn't remembered?

Tom realized in that moment just how important managing
expectations can be—and that people will sometimes forget. He
needed something that would stick in people's minds to help
them remember "3 up, 1 down."

The street in front of Tom's office was paved with bricks tightly
jammed together. Bricks often loosened or pieces chipped free.
An idea came to him. He could use bricks to help clients remember "3 up, 1 down." He created what is commonly referred to as

the "brick through the window story." To help people remember what they should expect with their investments, the following story is now told across America to thousands of potential investors.

> Once out of every four years you should expect your investments to go down in value. During that year you may get upset with me. As a matter of fact, you may get so mad at me that you want to do something drastic, like *throw a brick through my window*!!! All I ask is that as you are standing out there in that street with that brick in your hand about ready to throw it through my window, you *attach a check*, because that is the best time to be adding to your investments. Always remember, "3 up and 1 down."

It worked. People remembered the brick through the window. At times, Tom would actually give them a brick, and most importantly, he would repeat the story multiple times to his clients and prospects. Remember, **just because you tell someone something once, it doesn't mean that they will remember**. Repetition is critical when it comes to managing expectations.

Flash forward five years—the Whalens had done so well with their saving and investing that they were featured on the front page of the business section of their local paper. They had retired and were going to tour the country to see their children and grandchildren regularly. They had achieved their goal.

The real key to managing expectations is telling people the good *and the bad* of what they should expect. Most people just flat out won't talk about the potential for negative outcomes. When someone will look you in the eyes and let you know the good and also the bad of what you should expect, there is an immediate bond of trust that is formed. Not to mention that the likelihood of future arguments has just been dramatically decreased.

Sounds like the ideal foundation for a relationship.

When you manage expectations, you create trust. And trust is the foundation of teamwork and, ultimately, performance. If you're a part of a team that doesn't have trust, you have a link, but that link is frayed. When you're placed under pressure, that frayed link is going to break.

How important is trust? It's the foundation of the training soldiers get in the US Army. The entire process of basic training is designed to give soldiers a sense of cohesion and trust with their teammates. In a 2000 article for *Military Review*, Major Robert J. Rielly called trust between soldiers "the single most sustaining and motivating force for combat soldiers."[2]

If trust and managing expectations is that effective under the stress of military conditions, just imagine what it can do for business organizations and families.

The term "trust" itself can come off as vague and abstract, but it's actually a concrete thing. You know when you have it, and you know when you don't. And it's something that can be built through a process. As you manage expectations—and establish that you can be trusted to do what you say you will do, when you say you will do it—you become more trusted. **Without trust, no team can succeed for long.**

THE WEIRD GUY ON THE BIKE

Years ago, Tom moved his family from St. Louis to Paducah, Kentucky, to begin his career as a financial advisor. On one of the first nights in their new home, he was just getting ready to sit down to dinner with his family when he heard a knock on the door.

Tom had spent the day introducing himself around to folks in the neighborhood and town, so he wondered if it might be one of the people he had met earlier.

When he opened the door, he saw that it was a man in a sweat suit, holding something in his hands. After a few seconds, Tom realized that he recognized the man. It was a guy he had seen riding his bike, seemingly aimlessly, in circles around the neighborhood that day. The man introduced himself and handed something to Tom—it was a plate with pieces of celery filled with cream cheese. He said, "Welcome to the neighborhood!"

Tom thanked the man and quickly closed the door. He walked to the kitchen and tossed the paper plate into the trash. He realized his heart was pumping because he had no idea how to interpret the "meeting." Was the man on the bike somebody to fear? Was he crazy?

You're probably wondering what a random interaction with a neighbor has to do with a chapter on managing expectations. We tell the story because it illustrates one of the fundamental misconceptions people have about "doing business."

You hear it all the time. People talk about wanting to establish relationships, or how it's "all about the relationship."

It needs to be much more than that. The term "relationship" is too vague.

After the guy on the bike dropped his present off at the house, he and Tom had a relationship. Sure, it was based on fear, but it was still a *relationship*.

The goal isn't just to have relationships. It's to build trusting and productive relationships. Relationships grow when trust grows. Think about the business relationships you develop successfully over time. How they start, and what they become. For the most part, relationships fall somewhere on a spectrum called the hierarchy of relationships.

DEPENDENCE
LOYALTY
TRUST
CREDIBILITY
SUSPICION
FEAR

DEPENDENCE: Do not want to be without the relationship
LOYALTY: A relationship of value is formed
TRUST: Belief that the relationship will bring value
CREDIBILITY: Hope that the relationship may bring value
SUSPICION: Concern that the relationship may cause harm
FEAR: Belief that the relationship will cause harm

When Tom first met the guy on the bike, the relationship was one of fear, at least on Tom's side. He didn't know why the guy was knocking on his door. Once it was clear the guy was harmless (but still a little off), the relationship graduated from fear to suspicion.

It's obviously your goal to move your business relationships into categories 4–6. The better you are at managing expectations, the more easily you will move up the ladder. Managing expectations fosters credibility, trust, and loyalty.

Let's put it into a real scenario that you can recognize from your day-to-day life. Let's say there's a quick oil change place you decide to use for the first time. You probably have three main concerns about the place: you want to make sure they're going to do a good job on your car, you want to know how long it's going to take, and you want to know how much it's going to cost.

The place looks clean and well-kept, so you go online and read reviews of the place. The shop is generally considered to be solid.

Whatever issues customers had, they said the company worked to resolve them quickly. Great, *credibility* is established.

You drive in, and the attendant tells you the service you need is going to cost $50 and will take thirty minutes. You are now somewhere between credibility and trust. You go to the waiting room while the work is being performed.

If the attendant comes back in twenty minutes and tells you that it turns out you didn't need some particular part of the service, so you're good to go early and for $40, you're probably going to go back to that shop again. Your level of trust in the shop has increased. They delivered what they said they would—even faster and cheaper than you expected.

Extend the metaphor out to having a new roof put on your house. You get a quote from the contractor, and he says it will take a week to do the work, and it will cost $5,000. And, by the way, it will be incredibly noisy and dusty for those seven days. When the contractor outlines the potential bad news of "noise and dust," it immediately increases credibility and trust.

If you come back from a week at your in-laws (to avoid the noise and dust), and the contractor hands you a bill for $5,000 and shows you a completed roof, you're happy and satisfied. *Trust* has been established. If he hadn't told you about the noise, and you had planned a conference call from your home office for one of those days, you may not have had the same opinion—even if the bill came in exactly as you expected and the contractor delivered on time. *Suspicion* is where the relationship now stands. Managing expectations only *partially* isn't a partial victory. It's a failure.

It's imperative to think about the most important areas where expectations should be managed. In professional relationships it is typically all about letting people know what they should expect in terms of service, cost, and time frames.

Is trust an absolute requirement within a team in order to win consistently? Absolutely! **People who don't trust each other cannot work together effectively.** Without trust, teams cannot win consistently, and in business, great teams become teammates with their clients.

MAKE MANAGING EXPECTATIONS A HABIT

The concept of managing expectations sounds great, but how do you actually do it? For leaders, this isn't some kind of abstract art. The mechanics of managing expectations happens on the ground, day by day. The metrics we're going to describe below aren't complicated, but they're rigorous. They're easy to understand, but following them every day will be a challenge.

When you do, you're putting yourself in the category to make winning a habit.

1. **Time:** The person who understands the value of time has a head start on those who don't. Time is generally the first impression, and being late starts any interaction with disrespect and broken trust. If you're late, you're sending the message that you don't care. People who are consistently late don't think this is a big deal, but for people who are consistently on time, it *is* a big deal. And it sets the late people on a track from which they almost cannot recover. In the Cardinals organization, it was understood that being on "Cardinal time" to a meeting meant you were fifteen minutes early. It was understood that this was what was required to show your respect for the other people in the meeting—and the material that was going to be covered. Arriving on time meant you were late, and being early was "on time."

2. **Service/Cost:** If you make a commitment or a promise, it is your obligation to deliver on it. People don't want surprises. The goal should be to think through very carefully what you can actually deliver, and then deliver it, in the time frame you committed to at the price you stated. It's imperative to also outline the potential for "worst-case scenarios." Let others know in advance what could happen and how you will handle it if everything doesn't go perfectly.

3. **Repetition, Repetition, Repetition:** Just because you managed expectations well for a week or a month or for one sale doesn't mean that everybody on your team or in your client pool heard it, understood it, and remembered it. You need to have repetition, consistency, and accountability. We often say that "managing expectations is a full-time job." You must do it repeatedly, and it needs to become a core part of your communication. How do you know when you're doing it right? Tom likes to call it the "Parrot Test." The best investment advisors are constantly reminding investors that they can expect one bad year for every three good ones. They say it so much that the clients can parrot the words back to them.

When it comes to managing expectations you must remember that great teams often develop two people at a time. Anytime there is communication between teammates, there is potential for increasing or decreasing trust. Every time trust is increased, the team becomes stronger. Trust is most commonly developed in one-on-one communication.

If this was something every person was doing already, we wouldn't have to have this conversation now. But the reality is, we're all human, and we come up short. Even if you work on the concepts we've been talking about, you're going to face situations where you mismanage expectations.

The answer isn't to paper over the mistake by ignoring it, or thinking it is just a blip. The most successful people and teams are completely accountable. No one is perfect—we all make mistakes. But when a mistake is made, don't make excuses for your short-comings. Even if there's a legitimate "excuse" for falling short on a deliverable—the projections changed, the raw materials didn't show up, a kid got sick, whatever—don't try to pin the responsi-bility somewhere else. It just diminishes trust even further when you make excuses. Instead, use the negative outcome as motiva-tion to perform at a higher level in the future.

What does taking ownership look like? The owner of a small marketing firm who is a client of Jason's serves as a great example. Many years ago the owner of the firm was over a week late getting payroll completed and checks out to his employees. Once he did get payments out, he took full responsibility for the mismanaged expectations of the timing of payday. He called a short meeting in which he looked each of his employees in the eyes and said the following, "I'm sorry, there is no excuse. I will work to make sure this never happens again." He then handed each employee his or her paycheck with an additional $10.00 included and a small note reading, "Please enjoy lunch on me as a small token of my appre-ciation for what you do for this company."

Over the years the boss noticed that when his employees made mistakes or came up short on what was expected, they often re-sponded with the same words he had chosen: "I'm sorry, there is no excuse. I will try very hard to make sure this never happens again." Over time, the no-excuse mentality has actually become a part of the culture. Pretty good for a small marketing firm that in the past ten years has grown its profitability from $700,000 yearly to now over $15 million.

Say you're a father with a son who has a basketball game on a weekday at 7:00 p.m. You've said you're going to come home from work in time to see the game, but work happens and you end up having to miss the game. You could pull your son aside later and say, "I'm sorry I missed the game. Something came up at work and I couldn't get away." That would be true, but what your son hears is "work is more important than me."

The accountable approach—the one that honors expectations—would be to say, "I'm sorry I can't make the game tonight. There's no excuse, and I'll work hard to do better in the future."

BUILDING TRUST

The feeling is almost universal. You're the new person, and you've been dropped into a team setting with a bunch of people you don't know. It could be attending a new university, signing on to a new sports team, or being switched to a different division in the workplace.

The goal in any of these situations is fundamentally the same. You want to establish yourself on the team and build real relationships with the people around you. You want them to like you; ultimately, you want them to trust you.

But the first—and completely natural—connection between people isn't friendship. It's suspicion. Humans are wired that way. We're cautious until we know more about what we're dealing with. We're wondering what's up with the guy on the bike, or the salesman walking toward us at the car dealership, or even the members of our new team at work. Are they allies, or are they rivals?

When you're suspicious, you question motives, and you have no reason to automatically trust what somebody says. How you bridge that gap and move on from suspicion determines how well you—or anybody else—can integrate with the team.

You move from suspicion to *credibility* when you can manage expectations. You do what you say you're going to do. It is almost exactly like the tryouts that happen before the season on a sports team. The new players come in and are asked to show what they can do. If they arrive on time and show some promise, they can make the team—but they have to integrate with the team and show they can do it consistently.

In the business world, it's the difference between getting the meeting and getting the business. When you get the meeting, the person you're sitting across from is telling you that he or she believes in you enough to hear you out. That's credibility. When that same client hands you a check, he or she is *taking action*, and that's a great indication that trust has been established.

What does credibility look like in a team setting in the business world? If you repeatedly do what you say you're going to do—managing expectations—your fellow team members will give you their time when you ask them to hear you out. In any organization, time is a form of currency—just like cash. If someone agrees to have a meeting with you, that person is validating your credibility. **If someone will not agree to a meeting or take the time to hear what you have to say, you haven't established your credibility.** They're still suspicious of you.

The next step after credibility is a big one—and it's the one that makes the difference between average organizations and teams and great ones. It's the step from credibility to trust.

When somebody trusts you, it means he or she will take action. You see it all the time in the relationship between spouses, or between parents and their children. Those are people you'd do anything for, because you trust them completely. It's why organizations often try to characterize themselves as "families"—because of all the trust that exists among close-knit family members. Trust happens when you know someone will get it done for you, no matter what. You trust someone when you know you can count on them.

Questions to cause you to think:

1. What is one company that I do business with that I "trust"?
2. What is the main reason I "trust" that company?
3. On a scale of 1–10, how much "trust" do I think people should have in my company or team?

Taking that giant step from credibility to trust is where the money is made in modern business. It's why thousands of people spend millions of dollars trying to train themselves into the best practices that make that leap a little easier. But it has been our experience that getting to trust takes time. And it takes longer in some cases than in others. The most achievable and controllable step is to focus on getting to credibility. If a person can get to credibility and then continue to manage expectations effectively, eventually trust will ensue. You can speed up the process of getting to trust, but it will take your best efforts. It comes from three steps:

1. **Endorsement:** When you apply for a job, what do you take with you? A resume. Why? Because a resume is effectively an endorsement for what you've done. It shows where you went to school, what you studied, and who can vouch for you. It's a way for somebody who has never met you to start to make some judgments about what you might be like. Moving from credibility to trust happens much more quickly and easily if you have an endorsement from a known party—like a live version of your resume, so to speak. The endorsement from a common associate gets you in the door—it gives you credibility. But to get from credibility to trust, you must then prove yourself.

2. **Value:** This is a term that gets thrown around more than almost any other in business circles. "Add value" and "value

proposition" are common catchphrases. Unfortunately, most people are more interested in what value they can get instead of what they can actually provide. It's essential for any team to know that the most important thing they can do for people is to help them. Be as concerned with helping others as you are with helping yourself. Once you promise value, then you absolutely must deliver. Serve others and yours will come.

3. **Honesty:** Honesty is an easy word to throw around. You'll find no shortage of organizations that are happy to tell you how squarely they'll deal with you and how honest they are. But truth telling is easy when times are good and the facts are in your favor. What happens when things aren't so great and you need to share bad news? If you resort to half-truths and exaggerations, you're going to lose trust. **Speaking the full truth won't always make you popular, but it will make you trustworthy.** Having the courage to be honest, especially when it's painful, speeds up the credibility process. Managing expectations properly is the highest form of honesty.

Loyalty and dependence grow from trust. Neither one forms without expectations that are managed properly over a meaningful period of time. When an individual—or a team—consistently manages expectations in all areas and delivers on substance, loyalty and dependence are more quickly developed.

Managing expectations is something that team leaders can teach their teams, and they can teach it not just through words, but also by example. When a team leader manages expectations, he or she is modeling how to do it. These habits lead to credibility and trust, both between team members and clients and among the team members themselves. When team members are able to manage expectations, they are valuable to the team. They build relationships with clients, and they build relationships within the team. All of this leads to a team performing at its best and becoming successful.

THE TRUTH ABOUT
MANAGING EXPECTATIONS

Let's use a little self-evaluation to get a sense of where you are with managing expectations.

1. Do I ever commit to being somewhere at a certain time only to show up late?

If you answered yes, then no matter what you have told yourself, this is not okay, and it's the first step of trust deterioration. The first step to overcoming lateness is to stop making excuses. Next time you are late, force yourself to say these words, "I'm sorry I am late. There is no excuse and I will work on this not happening again."

After saying those words, you will then want to say, "But let me just explain what happened." This is called "falling into the trap of the viable excuse." Do not allow yourself to go there. Even if there is a valid excuse, you will be better off owning the mistake fully. This is where true growth occurs, and people will respect that you are not one of those "excuse makers."

If you are a person who is consistently on time and who meets deadlines, be very proud of yourself. It is a tremendous sign of respect and integrity and certainly the mark of a highly successful person. Continuing to be on time not only keeps you on track for success but contributes greatly to creating the environment for success at work and with your family and personal relationships.

2. On a scale of 1–10, how honest am I with people (even when sharing bad news)?

If you answered anything less than a 10, this is an area of opportunity for you. Get in the habit of thinking about situations where people may have questions about what they should expect from you or what you can do for them. Anytime you feel there may be uncertainty, that means you must put effort into managing expectations. Let people know exactly what they should expect, whether they are clients or fellow team members. Remember, managing expectations about the potential for good outcomes is important. But managing expectations about the potential for negative outcomes is *essential*.

If you answered a 10 on the question above, excellent work: you are a true master of managing expectations.

TEACH IT

The hierarchy of relationships:

DEPENDENCE
LOYALTY
TRUST
CREDIBILITY
SUSPICION
FEAR

DEPENDENCE: Do not want to be without the relationship
LOYALTY: A relationship of value is formed
TRUST: Belief that the relationship will bring value
CREDIBILITY: Hope that the relationship may bring value
SUSPICION: Concern that the relationship may cause harm
FEAR: Belief that the relationship will cause harm

The more effective you are at managing expectations, the faster you will create credibility and trust.

INVERT

(By inverting any fundamental you can learn more)

Managing expectations is the fastest way to build trust and credibility; not managing expectations is the fastest way to drain trust and credibility.

"3 MOST IMPORTANT" FOR THE TEAM TO REMEMBER

1. Managing expectations means you tell people up front exactly what they should expect and then you deliver—NO EXCUSES.
2. All breakdowns in personal and professional relationships are a result of expectations not being managed effectively.
3. Managing expectations is a full-time job and should be done repeatedly and consistently.

"1 MUST" TAKEAWAY FOR TEAMS

It is essential in business to manage expectations about time, service, and costs. Effectively doing so with the potential for positive outcomes is good, but including the potential for negative outcomes is even more important.

Chapter 3

SELF-EVALUATION: THE GENESIS OF ALL IMPROVEMENT

Self-Evaluation: Self-assessing how well you are doing

How important is evaluation? Benjamin Franklin, one of the most successful individuals in American history, considered daily self-examination to be an "absolute necessity" for personal improvement. How about for the team and its members?[1]

It may be true that absolutely no improvement—and yes, we mean zero—can happen without self-evaluation. Evaluation of others is important, but *self*-evaluation is the real key. We believe self-evaluation is the genesis of *all* improvement.

It's one thing to let someone else know how they are doing. It's a completely different ball game to have a person think for themselves about what they are doing well and what they need to improve.

The Cardinals had one of the game's legendary pitching coaches in Dave Duncan. Dunc was famous for his ability to take a player who had underperformed on a different team and rebuild him into a valuable contributor who pitched to the peak of his potential.

The World Series Championship rosters of the Cardinal teams from 2006 and 2011 are filled with those reclamation project pitchers, and they got some of the most important outs the team needed during those years.

How did Dunc do it?

One of the pitchers in question told Jason the secret: "Dunc doesn't get in my face and tell me what I need to do," he said. "He asks me what I think will help, and what one change I can make that will go the right direction. He makes me come up with it. Then I try it, and if it works, great. If not, he asks me to come up with another idea. At some point, if my ideas aren't working, I'll ask him and he'll give a few suggestions, but I always have to come back and tell him what I think. He is always making me figure out what I need."

After Jason saw this transformation happen time and time again, he came to realize that the strategy was just as effective for players who were *already* high-level performers as it was for players trying to get to their peak. It let all of the players participate in the process of becoming the best possible version of themselves.

How is this different from standard coaching? A regular coach will deliver information to the player and tell him or her to go work on it. That's fine, and it will work to a certain degree—especially if the coach is an expert. But when the coach can deliver information that helps the player perform better, and also gets players to evaluate the results themselves—by asking questions—the results are compounded.

Why?

Because when you participate in the process, you get more than just knowledge. You get conviction. You have a more concrete belief in the process. You're invested.

Jason later came to phrase this concept as **"Conviction beats expertise seven out of ten times."** Telling someone what he or she needs to improve can be helpful, especially if you are an expert in the area of discussion. Asking the right questions and getting the person you are teaching or coaching to identify the needed improvement is much more effective.

Conviction is better than knowledge: conviction is motivation. Where there is motivation, there is generally action. And conviction is developed through self-evaluation.

We've worked with hundreds of businesses in nearly every category over the past several years, and even though they have different missions and structures, the best ones have remarkably similar attitudes about their people. They know that they need to create an environment for high achievers to be recognized and energized so they can move up quickly in the organization.

One of our common tasks is to come in and help create plans and programs that will support those high achievers. A few years back, we were asked to spend a year working with a select group of thirty promising young talents at a Fortune 100 company. One of the first tasks we asked the group to do was to take no more than sixty seconds every day to write down on paper the three things they did well in the previous twenty-four hours.

Notice we said "on paper." That's important, and intentional. Typing it on your phone—or thinking about it in your head— doesn't form the same connection with the information as physically writing it down. The act of writing makes it real—literally and figuratively.

Slowly but relentlessly, every person in the group started experiencing a change in mindset—even the ones who initially thought it was silly to be writing stuff like that down. We're talking about a set of aggressive, high-achieving, Type-A folks. At the beginning, they were very ready to be critical of themselves if they made a mistake. That's not a good idea—negative thinking doesn't get processed the right way, and it gets in the way of your performance. Your negative thoughts actually keep you from recovering from your mistakes as quickly.

As the positive self-evaluations kept coming in, the people in the group not only continued to survive challenging scenarios in their roles, but started thriving on the challenges. Other team members began looking to them for support and advice, and by the end of the year, the average increase in production for each member of the group was more than 30 percent.

Over the course of a year, we obviously worked on more than just writing the "done wells" down on paper. Make no mistake, though: that is where we start with every person we coach. **Learning to evaluate what you do well is the first fundamental of developing mental toughness.** Rule number one, with all evaluation, is to *always* start with the positive. It sets the right tone for open-mindedness and builds on strengths rather than tearing down self-confidence.

It can't be that simple, you're thinking.

It actually can, and it is. How you frame a situation in your own mind is the strongest determining factor in the first step you will take in response to the situation. If you're negative, bored, tired, aggravated, or resigned to something going wrong, your attitude and performance are already compromised. It's the difference between Carol Dweck's fixed and growth mindsets. Carol Dweck is a research psychologist who specializes in motivation. A fixed-mindset person sees something as good or bad, on a basic scale. The growth-mindset person sees opportunities for learning and improvement whether things are going wrong or right.[2]

THE OBSESSION FOR IMPROVEMENT

When Jason started with the St. Louis Cardinals, his job was to help players and coaches develop the mental toughness needed to win a World Series.

One of the cornerstones of the mental training program he built as the director of sport psychology was called the "Success Log." Within sixty minutes of the last pitch of every game, players were tasked with writing down the answers to three questions:

1. What three things did I do well in the game?
2. What one thing do I want to improve in the next game?
3. What is one action step I can take to make that improvement?

Players started working on this brand of self-evaluation in 2006, and the Cardinals won the World Series that year for the first time since 1982. More and more players bought into the program—and the team won the title again in 2011.

The beauty of the tool is that it works as well for leaders and managers as it does for team members.

THE THREE BIGGEST
SELF-EVALUATION MISTAKES

Most people self-evaluate, but unfortunately, they do it incorrectly. The real trick is to get people asking themselves the right questions—evaluating effectively. The processes we describe here are relatively simple, but that doesn't mean that things won't go wrong—or that you won't have some roadblocks in your self-evaluation practice. We've been able to group almost all of the common issues into three categories. When you run into those problems, look below to understand how to quickly give yourself the boost you need to get back on track.

1. **Perfection vs. Improvement: When you emphasize improvement over perfection, progress accelerates.** Many people—especially high achievers—have come to equate a "solution" to a problem as "complete resolution." In other words, if something isn't done perfectly or completely, it isn't a solution. This perfectionist mentality drains the energy from teams because it often puts people in a position where they feel like they've failed—even though they've improved. We like to fight this mentality with something called the "+1 Concept." Redefine your concept of a "solution" to include anything that produces improvement. Through a certain action, have you made something one percent, one step, or one "piece" better than before? This reframing lets the team be open to the concept of incremental improvement—team members are far less likely to give up, because their decisions and efforts continue to matter.

2. **Results over Process: The more you focus on results, typically, the harder it is to achieve those results.** That's known as "the paradox of the product goal." One of Jason's baseball clients was pitching a no-hitter for six innings. He was cruising along, thinking only about his process—stay back, arm on top, pound down in the strike zone. But when he got to the seventh inning and saw the scoreboard—which showed he hadn't given up a hit—he began thinking about throwing the no-hitter. Instead of focusing on his process, he started counting the outs he had left. By the eighth inning, he had given up a hit and two walks, and was

pulled from the game. The most common way people measure themselves is by results. What does the scoreboard say? What are the sales figures? How much did the company make? But the highest achievers don't focus most of their attention on those metrics. They define success by effort and adherence to the process. Your mind can only fully focus on one thing at a time. If your thoughts are focused on the results, you literally cannot be thinking about what causes the results.

3. **Negative over Positive: That which you focus on expands.** There is an old saying, "Positive thinking doesn't always work, but negative thinking does." It's totally normal to go right to what went wrong and pick that as your place to evaluate. Make no mistake, no matter what, with evaluation, your team will benefit greatly by *always* starting with the positive. If a football team commits two turnovers, the coach is going to want to figure out why those mistakes happened. Problems do need to be addressed, but if you focus your energy on the negative outcomes and don't give time to what you've done well, you will be increasing the likelihood for future mistakes. Instead of focusing on what went wrong, put energy into evaluating what went well and what will make it even better in the future. This small shift in thinking will make a world of difference in outcomes.

HOW THE BRAIN WORKS

Mental toughness is the ability to focus the mind on solutions, especially in the face of adversity. For mental toughness to occur, there are three very important things to consider.

First, it is totally normal for people to focus on problems. This is called PCT, or problem-centric thought. **PCT is the biological**

tendency to focus on the negative. Because of how our brains are built, it is totally normal to put more emphasis on what is going wrong than on what is going right. Think about it this way: Oxygen is the most valuable resource known to our species. But when is the last time you thought to yourself, as you were taking a breath, "This is awesome. I have the most valuable resource known to my species in seemingly infinite supply." Our guess is that you haven't recently had that thought. Compare that with the frequent thoughts of "I don't have enough money, love, or respect." That is where the mind goes naturally, and that is an example of PCT.

The second point you want to remember for mental toughness is expectancy theory. In simple terms, expectancy theory states that what you focus upon expands. As a human being, you're made up of thoughts, feelings, and behaviors, and your thoughts control how you feel and behave. If you focus your thoughts on negative things and personal shortcomings, that will have a negative impact on how you feel and how you behave, whereas **if you can train yourself to focus on those things you do well, the likelihood increases that you will feel better and take more positive action**.

The third consideration is self-confidence. Self-confidence is the number one variable for human performance. If self-confidence is high, that is the number one predictor for future success. If self-confidence is low, the likelihood for future success is low.

Great teams understand that self-evaluation, when done correctly, is the actual training mechanism for developing mental toughness. Mental toughness will not and does not happen without training. Self-evaluating your "done wells" daily, as well as how to improve your performance, actually creates neural patterns that cause self-confidence to increase and success to rise. You will feel much more "in control," and that is a very good thing for self-confidence and performance.

THE ART OF EVALUATION

Knowing that self-evaluation is important is the first big step. And learning to do it correctly is the next big step. Let's start with a pop quiz. Get a piece a paper and write down your answers to the following questions.

1. How often do I truly evaluate what I am doing?
2. What is the single most crucial thing that I should evaluate each day?
3. When have I discussed what I should be evaluating with my team leader/supervisor?

These questions aren't designed to discourage you, but we'll bet that you didn't have good answers (or any answers) to one or two of them. The goal is to design an effective and efficient self-evaluation process that keeps you in touch with the critical drivers of your success with enough frequency that you can learn and grow.

When we work with organizations on this mission, the first thing many of them expect is for us to give them some big, cumbersome tool they have to spend hours in a workshop learning how to use.

That can't be further from the case.

The best evaluations take just a few minutes, and they're the result of just a few questions. As we described with Jason's Success Log, they get right to the heart of the matter, and they identify the critical drivers.

In a business or team setting, you want to start at the top of the pyramid. Within your team, what is the single most important thing that must get done? That action is the first thing you need to evaluate. Most teams will answer this question with a result focus, and that's a great place to begin. Be certain when evaluating to always boil success down to the single most important action that is causing the results.

The best coaches and corporate leaders focus on these elements because they're *controllable*. A PGA Tour golfer can focus on his practice routine, his workouts, and his mental process before hitting each shot. He can't control what other players do, or what scores they shoot. If he does everything he should do, he has succeeded—no matter what the scores show. If he does everything he can and should do, but considers himself a failure, because he shot a score two shots higher than the winner, he's destined for an incredibly unsatisfying and underperforming life.

Anytime your team experiences success in results, be certain to ask the question "What is the single most important thing I am doing to cause these results?" **When you identify the cause of success, you increase consistency.** The success becomes much more repeatable.

A basic example within the framework of a sales team might be the number of consultations each team member initiates in a given week. If meeting with five new people in a week is the goal, then you need to evaluate the most important action step you're taking toward that goal. The natural temptation is going to be to take a deep dive into what you do and try to evaluate everything—but remember what we've been saying about channel capacity. Pick out a few things (three at the absolute most) that are the most critical. We've trained financial advisors, for example, to pick two simple metrics—the number of people each advisor speaks with in person and the number of client contacts daily.

When you create a short series of pointed questions, as in Jason's Success Log, you won't be giving yourself room to tiptoe out of your responsibilities by shading your answers. As Coach John Wooden used to say, "Don't mistake activity for achievement." Just because you're doing a bunch of stuff doesn't mean you're doing the *right* stuff.

Another natural inclination is to pick the big, obvious waypoints in your business as the right time to do evaluations. Looking back on what you do every quarter, every month, or every other week is nice and clean, but it doesn't make the best use of the tools we're talking about. Short and effective evaluations (three minutes maximum) done frequently (daily) speeds up the process of success.

WHERE DO YOU START?

You can bet that the great coaches and leaders are constantly evaluating the players on their roster (and potential players joining the team). But they're not just evaluating players' performance; they're evaluating their own systems and processes, to make sure they're first-rate.

What really happens in these high-achieving organizations is that they evaluate the *right* information, and they create a *culture* of self-evaluation. They reinforce what will be evaluated—and what steps are necessary for success as defined by the team—and they establish that it is important for individuals to evaluate themselves and hold themselves accountable for the tasks and processes on their plate.

Sports can be a useful metaphor because the results are right there in front of us every season. Players go into the draft and are evaluated. Teams choose who they think is the best fit. Rosters are managed in the preseason. Some players make the team and some don't. Teams win and lose games and are evaluated internally and externally. By coaches. By the media. By fans.

If you can build a culture of effective *self-evaluation*—either for your organization or for your team (or within yourself, if you aren't the one calling the shots)—and build a system that makes a ritual of those evaluations, you create an environment of consistent improvement and continual growth.

What are those "3 Most Important" activities each day that individuals need to focus on the most, and of the three, what is the "1 Must" that absolutely has to happen for the team to win? Resist the temptation to evaluate everything, because it's easy to fall into that trap. Honor channel capacity. Pick out three things, at most, that are crucial and critical.

Here are three self-evaluation questions that have proven to be very helpful in developing mental toughness, focus, and confidence in the business world.

1. What three things did I do well in the previous twenty-four hours?
2. On a scale of 1–10, how well did I do in the past twenty-four hours completing my "3 Most Important" tasks and "1 Must" task?
3. What is one thing I want to improve in the upcoming twenty-four hours?

WHEN TO EVALUATE

It's important to understand that evaluation needs to be something that is happening continuously, not just as a part of the specific performance evaluations every organization does every quarter or every year to measure and reward employees.

If you're waiting for these annual or quarterly reviews to implement these strategies, you're doing it wrong—and you're not taking full advantage of the tool. The normal performance evaluation consists of a manager telling a team member what the team member did, where he or she stands, and what is expected of the team member in the next segment of time. That's certainly important and helpful, but most of the time the team member isn't internalizing the advice—and isn't learning about what turns advice into action.

By creating a system that requires team members to self-evaluate regularly, performance reviews will just be one more reference point on a continuous process of improvement. Self-evaluation is such a powerful and effective method of driving improvement that it makes no sense whatsoever not to do it regularly. We strongly recommend taking, at most, three minutes per day to self-evaluate with the three questions from the previous page.

Highly successful teams use self-evaluation daily. The best teams honor channel capacity by identifying, at most, three effective self-evaluation questions to use, and then—to repeat—using them daily.

Doing so will create the "culture of evaluation" we are talking about. **Completing self-evaluations daily trains the mind to be in self-evaluation mode.** The result of self-evaluating daily is that team members and leaders alike will begin completing what we call *mini-evaluations*.

MINI-EVALUATIONS

The most successful people are in a constant evaluation mode. They perform a series of mini-evaluations multiple times per day. Coach Belichick has famously said that if you wait until halftime to make your adjustments, it's already too late.

By evaluating yourself on a small scale more often, you're better able to make corrections when you get off course—and everybody gets off course. Coach Wooden was one of Tom Bartow's mentors, and Tom once asked him what he would watch for during a game. What were his mini-evaluations? He answered, "I wanted to see what kinds of cuts my players were making. I wanted those cuts to be in sharp, straight lines, because straight-line cuts are quicker."

If the cuts were happening the way he liked, it meant that other good things within the plan were more likely to be happening.

What does a day look like when you're self-evaluating well? A few times—two or three—during the day, you're doing a twenty-second or so check-in with yourself. Simply ask yourself, "What is one thing I am doing well so far today, and what is one thing I want to improve?" When you get to the midpoint of your day, you can then spend another twenty seconds to evaluate your activity and achievement. Near the end of the afternoon, do a more comprehensive evaluation of your day by answering all three of the questions listed on page 62 and identifying your "3 Most Important" and "1 Must" for the next day.

By structuring the evaluations in this way, you're building a habit. It's no different from going to the gym or eating decent food. It isn't particularly hard on any one given day—the difficult and important part is doing it consistently.

Every team gets off course; through mini-evaluations, the highly successful get back on course much more quickly.

THE CULTURE OF SELF-EVALUATION

Creating a culture of effective self-evaluation is essential for improvement. This will occur only if self-evaluation is ritualized. As a leader, you must ensure that self-evaluation is happening on a regular basis and that the evaluation is effective.

Performance evaluations are a part of every successful organization. Unfortunately, most organizations aren't taking full advantage of them. The normal performance evaluation consists of the superior telling individual team members what they have done and where they stand. Undoubtedly this is a helpful process. However, until the individual internalizes the direction, it is just advice.

Think back to when you were a teenager and your parents gave you advice. Did you always internalize what they were saying? Until people say to themselves, "Yeah, you know, I really do need to make some changes," the advice is just advice. Unfortunately, **knowing something does nothing, but *doing* something does**.

Remember, conviction beats expertise seven out of ten times. Develop conviction by asking questions that promote self-evaluation. Get in the habit of putting in every performance evaluation a few questions that will cause self-evaluation. Don't just expect your team to self-evaluate: make certain that they do.

At its most basic definition, the concept of evaluation has been drummed into every manager's head since the beginning of his or her executive career. That can be a good thing or a bad thing, depending on how you define and execute evaluation.

What we're designing here is a culture. A culture where evaluation is constantly ongoing—and where it's happening within each member of the team. If you can instill that quality into your people, you're creating an army of team members who know the goals, understand the processes, and are liberated to think for themselves about how to improve the team every day.

We aren't suggesting that you create the expectation that multiple self-evaluations must occur throughout the day. The point we are making is that **if a person commits to self-evaluation one time daily, then the result is that people will naturally begin doing the mini-evaluations much more frequently on their own**.

SELF-EVALUATION ACCOUNTABILITY

The dynamic between peers on a team is obviously different from the manager–team member dynamic, and it means you need to use different strategies to get the most out of the evaluation process. When you're in the trenches with somebody, you can see things that might be lost on somebody even one level up the corporate food chain—and you understand what kinds of things might be important for the person next to you at the table.

Your goal is to leverage this business intimacy and help push the people on the team to see, measure, and achieve their goals. It comes from asking the right questions.

Everybody on the team—from the leader to the newest team member—should be doing the individual day-to-day self-evaluations we've been talking about. But the members of the team should also add in a kind of long-range evaluation and planning conversation three to four times a year. Pick a partner who is at roughly the same level as you on the team, and sit down and ask each other these questions.

Remember, write down your answers.

1. What were your three biggest personal accomplishments in the past three months? What were the team's three biggest accomplishments?
2. If you could go back and do three things differently, what would they be?
3. What is the number one most important thing you want to get accomplished in the next three months?

Why should you do this with a partner? Because seeing the answers will help you learn even more about how another person on your team thinks. You'll see how he or she prioritizes things, and what he or she sees as a success or failure. Many of the answers will probably be familiar, but you'll also be surprised by some of them.

Spend the most time talking about the accomplishments and what specific actions made them happen. It's like having a mini-best-practices seminar, where a peer can learn some new strategies to handle a particular problem that he or she might not have considered before.

Once you get to the last question, about priorities, it's a great way to find alignment on the team. If the priorities are different, why are they different? Maybe that's a natural part of the business. But it also might mean that one team member or the other has a misunderstanding about what the true goal is. It's an opportunity for the team to identify these misalignments and fix them in a way that isn't confrontational. You're not arguing in the middle of the game, but working out strategy ahead of time. This creative tension is productive and necessary for any organization to grow.

TEACH IT

Next time your self-confidence is low, force yourself to write down on paper three things that you have done well. Doing so will break the cycle of negative thinking and get you thinking more like a champion.

INVERT

(By inverting any fundamental you can learn more)

If you want your team to get off course and stay off course, don't evaluate.

"3 MOST IMPORTANT" FOR
THE TEAM TO REMEMBER

1. Self-evaluation builds conviction, and conviction promotes action.
2. Self-evaluation is the genesis of all improvement.
3. Rule number one with all evaluation is, *always* start with the positive.

"1 MUST" TAKEAWAY FOR TEAMS

On a daily basis, ask people to answer the following three questions:

1. What three things did I do well in the previous twenty-four hours?
2. On a scale of 1–10, how well did I do in the past twenty-four hours completing my "3 Most Important" and "1 Must" tasks?
3. What is one thing I want to improve in the next twenty-four hours?

Part II

Playoff Level

Reaching the playoffs is a milestone. Discover how to move your team from wanting to win to knowing how to win. Chapters 4, 5, and 6 are a necessity for championships.

Chapter 4

TURNING TEAM CHEMISTRY INTO TEAM COHESION

Team Cohesion: The sense of unity and purpose that emerges when each team member knows exactly where the team is going and attacks his or her role daily to create team success

"Chemistry" is a term you hear all the time in sports and business. Such and such team doesn't have players as good as those on the other team, but they win because they have great chemistry. Or a team is struggling because they have problems in the locker room. They don't have great chemistry.

In business, we hear it when we're working with leaders in charge of building sales teams. They wonder if they've made the right moves to create "chemistry" on their teams, because if the people in each group aren't friends, going out and doing fun stuff all the time, they won't do well.

Nonsense.

Sure, teams can be close-knit groups of friends. There's nothing wrong with that if it happens. But that usually isn't the case, and it certainly isn't a requirement. Some of the highest-performing teams we've been around in sports and business weren't friendly outside the lines. But inside the lines, when the score counted, they worked unbelievably well together.

Instead of chemistry, they understood and practiced team *cohesion*. The key ingredient is that there is direct alignment between the team's success and each individual's success. It's critical that when the players do their jobs, the team does well, and when the team does well, it benefits the players. Oftentimes it happens that people don't have clarity or agreement on their vision, and so the aspect of working to figure it out is disregarded.

Let's be clear: **no team, whether it be a marriage, a football team, or a corporate organization, experiences true high-level success without disagreements**.

Expectations must be managed here. There will be disagreements, and those disagreements are necessary. It will require great effort to achieve resolution. It's the work required to move through the disagreement that eventually becomes the glue that binds and creates cohesion.

Just as when a bone breaks and then knits itself back together, a team always grows stronger when its members work through disagreements.

The key is to be certain there is clarity about the team's vision, and specifically, about what is needed from each individual player in order for the team to experience the benefits resulting from consistent execution.

We're going to talk about what it takes to improve the group dynamic when it comes to *production*, not perception.

Why do organizations build teams in the first place? Because they're interested in increasing the performance they could expect if they just relied on each team member to do his or her thing independently. The sum is greater than the individual parts. They're trying to leverage systematic human performance.

And what do you think is the number one variable for human performance—whether we're talking about a team setting or individuals?

It's self-confidence.

When the players on a team—an NFL team, a sales team, an ambulance team, it doesn't matter which—walk onto the field with the knowledge that they're well prepared and that their teammates are the same, they will have confidence. The team will be positioned for success.

Let's talk about how to get there.

GOAL COMMONALITY

The first order of business is to identify the primary outcome or goal of bringing everyone together. For teams to work at the highest level, everyone in the organization must have this "goal clarity." Unfortunately, this is not very often the case.

In fact, as Stephen Covey reported in his book *The 8th Habit*, only 37 percent of individuals have a clear understanding of what the team is trying to achieve, and only 20 percent are enthusiastic about the team's goals. This would suggest that if you are on a team of fifteen people, only six members of that team know the goals, and only three are enthusiastic about them.[1]

Can you imagine a football or basketball team trying to win a championship with anything less than 100 percent of the players sharing the common goal of being world champions? How about if the players or coaches aren't enthusiastic about winning? It's almost laughable to think about.

It is every bit as important for teams in the business world to have a shared goal. There is much talk about teams having elaborate vision statements that clearly define everything the team is trying to accomplish. Vision statements can be a great way to ensure there is goal commonality and clarity. If your team has a well-defined vision statement, that's great—keep using it.

Unfortunately, many vision statements don't honor channel capacity. Vision statements often list multiple goals and objectives, leaving people confused about what is absolutely the most important part of the vision.

We are not suggesting that your team must have a vision statement. Not at all. In fact, we don't have strong opinions either way on this. We have seen successful organizations that use vision statements, and also successful ones that don't.

The point we are making is that whether you have a vision statement or not, make certain that your team has clarity around one product goal and one vision goal. A product goal is your most important result-oriented goal that can be achieved in the next twelve months. A vision goal is also a result-oriented goal, but with a longer time frame for accomplishment. A vision goal is the most important goal the team wants to achieve in three years or longer.

Product goals help keep people locked in on what's most important right now, and vision goals help people stretch a bit. It's important to note that most people still believe that when setting goals, it's good to follow the "set it high and hope to get close" approach. Unfortunately, there is no empirical evidence that this approach is effective, unless it is with goals with a time frame of three years or longer. Vision goals are good with longer time frames because they cause people to dream big and open their minds to what is possible.

Typically, when teams set shorter-term product goals (of one year or less) that are unrealistic, they get two or three months into the year and realize they are progressing at a pace well below what they need to be doing if they are going to reach the goal on time. Then they realize they will need to produce at an even higher pace to catch up. To avoid the stress and anxiety of underperforming, the internal defense mechanism causes people to forget about the goal altogether. **Unrealistic goals require unrealistic effort.** Unrealistic effort is very difficult to sustain for extended periods of time. Inconsistency and burnout are often the result of setting unrealistic goals.

Performing without goals is like flying a plane blindfolded and without instrumentation—not a good idea!

When it comes to product goals (again, with a time frame for achievement at no more than twelve months), try to set goals that are "realistically high." A simple rule to follow is to grow somewhere between 10 and 20 percent yearly. We have seen that teams that choose to set product goals in this range are much more likely to consistently hit the goal, which creates great self-confidence. Highlighting only one product goal and one vision goal honors channel capacity and keeps your team focused on what is absolutely most important. Setting realistically high goals fosters the habit of winning.

A financial services firm, for instance, may have a product goal of reaching $1 billion in assets under management and a vision goal of doubling EBITDA (a widely used measure of earnings) within five years. A baseball team may have a product goal of making the playoffs this year and a vision goal of winning the title within three years.

Once the goals are set, be certain to explain to team members why those goals are important and how hitting those goals will benefit the team and its members. Like it or not, we are built to care about ourselves. It's in our DNA. You can try to fight this, or you can accept it. There is an old Zen saying: "When faced with a powerful force, use the force to your advantage."

Personal survival is a powerful force. By creating business models where the team and the individuals win together, motivation aligns. Most organizations are already set up this way. What's missing is the clarity of how the team's success benefits the individual. Take the time to clearly explain to people how they prosper when the team wins.

When team goals are realistic and clear, and the benefits of success are clear for all team members, there won't be nearly as many cowboys off to the side doing their own thing, or divas sitting in the corner pouting. **When everybody is rowing in the same direction toward the same destination, you create the conditions for cohesive teamwork.**

ROLE INTEGRITY

Critical tasks need to be completed for teams to reach their most important goals. This becomes extremely important at the most practical level: the best teams have what's called *role integrity*.

When you look at a team and the assignments it has, what you should find is that all the team members have well-defined roles to play in achieving the stated team goals. Conversely, every task the team must accomplish in order to achieve the stated goals must have someone responsible for making sure it gets done. If there is a certain task that must be performed for the team to be successful, and the team doesn't have a person for that role, the team has a serious problem. Every important need the team has must be filled; if there is no one to fill a certain role, there will be crucial gaps in the work that gets done, and that will hold the team back.

A baseball team makes for a great analogy. The team's overall goal is to win the World Series. For that to happen, the team needs to have strong defense on the field for every game. There are nine positions out on the field, and nine different players must fit together to form the defense. The players have to be in the right positions, and they all have to be clear about which part of the field they're supposed to cover. If you have a weak or compromised player in one of those positions, there's a gap—or open space—in the defense, and it will be easier for opposing hitters to get on base successfully.

On any team, those kinds of gaps erode confidence, and they hurt the sense of teamwork. On a sales team with a variety of products in a portfolio, being short a person with expertise in a very important product in that line is damaging to confidence: it creates "gaps," a subconscious sense that the team will have a hard time meeting its goals.

The best organizations develop teams where there are no significant gaps when all team members are executing their jobs as expected. A critical step in creating role integrity is making sure all the team members know, within their given roles, what their "3 Most Important" and "1 Must" activities are daily. If all the players nail their "3 Most Important" and "1 Must" at least 90 percent of the time, there is continuity in the team's ability to perform and deliver.

When this happens, the team will win, and it will win consistently. This is in our experience the number one most critical variable for teams that consistently win. *This* is real team cohesion—not the fact that two or three people who sit near each other like the same kinds of movies and have kids in the same grade at school.

Patriots players Tom Brady and Rob Gronkowski couldn't have more different lives. Brady is married to a supermodel, has children, and eats an extremely strict diet to stay in prime shape. Gronkowski enjoys the single life and a few beers, and he isn't afraid to let loose. They're different, and off the field they don't really socialize. But when it comes to practice and game day, they're as close as anybody could be, because they know they can count on each other to always get the most important things done daily for their common goal.

Although having team members nail their "3 Most Important" and "1 Must" at least 90 percent of the time isn't complicated, let us assure you, it will not be easy. The good news is that you can help create the conditions for success with what we call *point and flow*.

POINT: THE ACT OF
RECOGNIZING ACHIEVEMENT

"Point" is exactly what it sounds like. You've seen it on the basketball court or in the backfield during a football game after a great play. The player who got the perfect pass from his teammate heads back up the court and points to the one who delivered the ball, or the person who gets the sack, high-fives the lineman who occupied two blockers and helped him get free.

It might seem like these are spontaneous reactions to an exciting play—and that's a little part of it. But they're also an extremely important part of reinforcing role integrity and execution. Players want to get the "point." It means they have been recognized for doing something that helps contribute to the team achieving its goal. It's a pure form of recognition for teamwork. It's the acknowledgment *from* the team that makes your individual contribution to the team more valuable.

It is recognizing the assist—the good work from a teammate.

How important is it? Coach John Wooden actually had his assistants chart the assists that players distributed during a game—and whether the player who received the pass acknowledged the passer after the basket. Players were actually graded on how well they pointed!

By now, you've heard us refer to New England coach Bill Belichick plenty of times as one of the premier leaders in sports and business. It won't surprise you to hear that the "point" is an important subject for him, too. Coach Belichick has stopped film study meetings cold and asked his team what was wrong with what looked to be a great defensive play. His linemen had recorded an important sack, and afterward, they were walking back to the line of scrimmage.

The problem? Nobody on the line had pointed, or recognized their teammates' contributions in any way. Coach Belichick knows that the only way to win consistently at the highest level is to recognize team cohesion when it happens.

We call this a *cultural element*, because it really needs to be something in your organization's DNA. We are not talking about the once-a-year awards ceremony. Although that is a great way to recognize success, the "point" needs to happen daily among team members. *Anytime* a person does something that contributes to the improvement of the team, even if it propels the team only an inch forward, it is point-worthy.

The concept of pointing out the assist needs to be immediate and frequent. Do this enough, and it starts to become automatic.

Think about it from the perspective of the team members. If you're the person who made the key pass, you're appreciative of the recognition for your efforts to help the team achieve the goal. If you're the point scorer, so to speak, it shows you appreciate the work that went in "behind the scenes," and it improves your relationship with the assist person. It increases the confidence of everybody involved, inspiring the team to commit to putting out the effort needed to receive more of the same kind of recognition.

Three questions to consider:

1. Has my organization clearly defined what behaviors are "point-worthy"?

2. When was the last time I "pointed" at a teammate for something he or she did well?
3. When was the last time a teammate "pointed" at me for something I did well?

THE "POINT" WITH CLIENTS

You don't need to be wearing the same jersey to use the "point" to bring value to the team. When Tom Bartow visits his dentist, the dentist compliments him on how well he's doing flossing his teeth. He often says, "Your flossing is costing me money." Tom certainly appreciates the "point," and it makes Tom want to keep flossing.

One of the techniques we coach our people on is something called the "2–1–1." It's a method of communication that's backed up by science, and it's proven to deepen relationships, increase credibility, and create a sense of team cohesion with clients.

Remember, **great teams make teammates out of clients**.

You begin the conversation by giving the client two genuine compliments, then you teach the client one thing, and then, finally, you coach the client on one action step. For example, the dentist might say to Tom, "You are doing a great job of flossing, and the fact that you are consistently coming into the office a couple of times every year for your cleaning and fluoride treatments is a really smart thing you are doing."

Those two compliments are the equivalent of "pointing" two times. The "point" deepens the relationship—in this case, the dentist's relationship with his patient, Tom—but it works with clients and teammates in the same way. When compliments are sincere, they are a terrific way to recognize positive behavior. **Genuine compliments lay the foundation for deepening relationships.**

It's quite common for those hearing the compliments to not know how to respond. Think about how foreign it is to have someone, anyone, give you a genuine compliment. It just doesn't happen very often—and when it does, oftentimes people don't know how to reply. You should expect this and be ready for it.

There are a few common responses you will get from people who are not used to hearing compliments. First, it is very common for someone to say, "I'm just doing what you told me to do." The recipient of the compliment isn't used to being complimented, so he or she is attempting to deflect it back to you. Do not let this happen. Remember, this is about telling the other person what he or she has done well, not about stroking your own ego. Do not let the recipient push the compliment off; otherwise, the "point" is not truly received, and the opportunity for recognition for a job well done is lost.

Respond to the "just doing what you told me" comment by saying, "I may have given you the idea, but it was you—you were the one who put it into action. I am not taking any of the credit for this, this was all you. Way to go." You could, in that instance, also go on to say, "I guess we just make a good team."

It's also common for someone to say, after receiving a compliment, "You gave me those same two compliments last month." A good way to respond is, "I'm glad, because you deserved those compliments last month every bit as much as you do this month. Keep it up!"

Genuine **compliments never get old.** The key is to make certain they are sincere and honest. If so, you can give those same compliments over and over and it will still make a very positive impact.

Once you have given a couple of genuine compliments, then you want to teach one thing that brings true value to the other person. This is the second part of the 2–1–1 method. Try to limit the teaching to things in your sphere of influence. Tom's dentist really shouldn't be teaching Tom about golf or racquetball. It might come off as the dentist trying to look like a know-it-all, and this will decrease Tom's motivation to listen to his dentist.

When teaching, the key is to truly bring value to the other person. Teach something that will improve the quality of that individual's life.

The dentist might say to Tom, for example, "I recently finished an article in one of our medical journals about the release of a new electric toothbrush. This toothbrush is the first of its kind because of its patented rotation of bristles. It has been clinically proven to reduce gum disease and cavities by an additional 12 percent over the leading electric toothbrushes on the market. It's like a toothbrush with super-powers."

When you teach something that brings value, you raise credibility. When credibility is increased, so, too, is the motivation to listen to you and to take action based on what you have said. Not to mention that you will become much more referable as your level of credibility increases. Teaching causes you to become "the expert."

The final part of the 2–1–1 conversation involves you coaching the other person in one action step that will cause that person to improve in some way. Action drives success. **When you motivate people to take positive action, they know you care.** The caring takes precedence over compensation. It becomes a relationship of "trust" rather than "suspicion."

The dentist could coach Tom by saying, "The one thing I would like you to do right now is to get those special toothbrushes for yourself and each family member. They have them up front and we get them at the price of $38.00. The money you spend today on those toothbrushes I am certain will save you a whole lot more on the other end in visits to me."

The 2–1–1 is an extremely effective method of communicating with team members, clients, and prospects. Allow us to give you a few more examples of how to use it.

If you are a financial advisor talking to a client, it could go something like this:

> In reviewing your portfolio, there a couple of comments I would really like to make. First off, you have done an excellent job of earning a strong income. The income you made last year puts you in the top 5 percent of income earners in the country. That is really impressive—you should be proud of that. Another thing you are doing really well is saving money each month. I'm not sure if you are aware of this, but when it comes to savings, the national average is typically a negative number. The fact that you're financially responsible enough to save every month, that is really a great thing you're doing. I know we may have covered this before, but it would be good for you to hear again: this is what I want you to remember, that what you should expect with your investments is that in every four-year period, your investments should go up in value three years and down in value one year. Just remember "3 up and 1 down." Now, based on the markets and your specific goals, the one thing you need to be doing right now is making sure you have the exact right amount and right type of insurance to fit your family's needs. Let's take a look at what you currently have.

If you are a nurse speaking to your supervisor, it could go like this:

> I was hoping I would see you this morning. I wanted to tell you how much I appreciated watching you with my patient last night. You were so caring, and it was so nice of you to go

out of your way to make sure she had those extra pillows. Not to mention that you sat and talked with her for ten minutes. I know that meant a lot to her and I wanted to thank you. I think it's good for you to hear that when we (the nurses) see things like that, it really shows us how to act with the patients. I have learned more from you about how to treat patients than I have from any book. And I don't know if it's out of line to ask this, but would you ever consider occasionally giving us presentations on how to better care for our patients? Even if you did it just once a month for ten or fifteen minutes I know it would be really helpful.

If you are a head football coach speaking to an assistant coach, you might say:

James, I just wanted to let you know you have been doing a great job with the team. You show up every day early and ready to go—the energy level you are bringing to practice is contagious, and that is very helpful. In addition, the scouting reports you have been providing are top-notch. You being on this team makes us a much better team. The one thing I want you to be aware of is that your star player (Chris) has a history of not being honest with the trainer and team doctor about his injuries. In high school he could get away with playing hurt, but that won't happen at this level. With this in mind, I would like for you to personally see to it that Chris is being honest with the medical staff. It might be a good idea for all of you to meet weekly together for updates. I know he trusts you, and if you are in those meetings I would feel much more confident that we have a better chance of keeping him healthy.

Learn to communicate with the 2–1–1 approach and you will immediately begin creating deeper and more cohesive relationships with coworkers and clients.

FLOW: PERFORMANCE
WITHOUT INTERRUPTION

The second method for creating positive conditions for team members nailing their "3 Most Important" and "1 Must" is what we call *flow*—another popular concept in the world of sports. When an athlete is "in the flow," it means he or she feels the rhythm of the game. Everything around the player seems to be moving slowly, and he or she can really take control on the field of play. The game seems easy, and the player can't wait to take the shot or make the play.

This flow state—the zone—is what every athlete is trying to find.

But flow isn't just about sports. It is just as possible for you to get in the flow at your desk job as it is for Dustin Johnson to do it on the golf course, or for Serena Williams to do it on the tennis court. You just need to identify what gets you there—and what the roadblocks are.

The best way to create "flow" in the business world is to totally attack your "1 Must" of the day without distraction. Interruptions are one of the biggest hindrances to getting into the flow state.

Think about it: when you are watching a basketball game and there are all kinds of starts and stops because of fouls being called or TV timeouts, you can see that at times it's really hard for players to get into the flow of the game.

The same is true for us in the business world. If you are trying to get your mojo going while performing your most important task of the day, and you keep having to take a phone call or answer emails, it's hard to get into that zone of optimal performance.

One of the most important things you can do to help create flow is to block out time in your schedule each day, first thing, to focus only on your most important task. Don't allow interruptions. Close your door (if you have one), and turn down the volume on your phone. Put a "Do Not Disturb" sign on your door and get your mind focused—even if only for a short period of time—on attacking your one most important thing.

Charlie Munger, vice chairman of Berkshire Hathaway, puts it this way: **"Many times it is more important to know what not to do than what to do."** Those in the business world should study Munger's advice thoroughly. He was referring to the necessity of streamlining your schedule so you can create flow and hyperfocus on what's most important.[2]

You have the usual suspects—meetings, conference calls, and many other kinds of nonessential interruptions that can take you from your focused place. One of the hazards of the modern cubicle configuration at many organizations is that it actually *encourages* people to get yanked out of their flow state. A person talks over the wall of the cube to ask you about the baseball game last night, or what you thought of the last episode of *Dancing with the Stars*. That's nice and friendly, but it's a flow killer.

You can also take yourself out of the flow by mishandling some of the time maximization skills we've discussed (here and in the original *Organize Tomorrow Today* book). If you aren't organized— if you're not clear about your priorities for the day and for the week—you're going to have a hard time finding the flow. And when you're distracted by things happening in your personal life, you're also going to struggle.

We're not looking for perfection here. The goal is to understand where most of the roadblocks come from, avoid them when you can—and acknowledge them when they happen. If you're clear-eyed about them, you can correct and move on as soon as possible. No matter what line of work you are in, interruptions will happen. Meetings, emails, and personal interests are the three most common interruptions. The overall goal, with any interruption, is to make it as short as possible.

In the workplace, you can't avoid meetings altogether: they're often required. But as a team, especially if you are the team leader, here are a few questions to consider when you are planning any given meeting:

1. Is the meeting necessary?
2. Will more than three points be covered in the meeting?
3. How could the meeting be shortened?

One of the purposes of a meeting should be to increase flow. If the interruption of having a meeting did not improve flow, you must ask yourself whether the meeting should have happened at all.

We have put great effort into making conference calls an art form. Our conference calls last no longer than nine minutes. On one occasion when there were only 250 total spots available to get on the call, all lines were full fifteen minutes before the call even began. In this organization, it had never happened before that a conference call was "sold out." People wanted to get on the call because they knew it would not be a distraction: it would be a catalyst. Only highly pertinent information was covered, and a clearly defined call to action was presented just prior to ending the call eight minutes and three seconds after it began.

Here are a few things to consider with meetings and conference calls:

1. The first rule should be: Don't talk just to fill time. Include only "red meat," by which we mean that the meeting or call should provide something solid that can be taken in and applied immediately to increase productivity and optimal performance. There should be no fluff.
2. The shorter the meeting or call the better. By the very nature of a conference call, you are fighting distractions. The computer screen is in front of the listeners, and they can mute their phones. Before the meeting or call begins, know how you will begin and end.
3. To increase listening intensity, tell the group in advance how long the meeting or call will be, but your goal should be to end before reaching the allotted time. When in doubt, end early.

There will obviously be interruptions in the workplace, no matter how focused the team. Almost everyone at times will need to break focus from work to make a call to the doctor, check in on a family member, or get online and check personal emails—or even surf the net. If you absolutely must interrupt your focus with personal interests, set a limit on the time you will allow yourself to be distracted.

Think of it this way: interruptions involving personal interests are the worst distractions. They are the complete opposite of team cohesion. Every minute you are focused on personal interests at work is literally a minute of team *not*-cohesion.

A good way to guard against distraction is to allow only one personal interest item at a time. For example, you might have multiple personal items that need to be taken care of. Only allow yourself time to take care of one item before getting something of professional importance completed. And when you are focused on that personal item, set a goal to never allow yourself more than four minutes of personal interest time at once. Then, maybe get to the second personal item after, and only after, some level of professional work has been completed.

CREATING FLOW

As stated above, the best method of creating flow is to attack the most important activity and to do it first. The first thing to remember is that as the day wears on, there will be more potential distractions. Coupled with that, for every hour that passes, your energy, focus, and discipline are decreasing. **Waiting until later in the day to get your most important activity completed is typically a recipe for inconsistency.**

Nailing, first thing, your most important activity of the day is an extremely effective way to get yourself and your team into the "zone." Think back to those days when you have gotten into the office and begun to attack your most important activity of the day from the start. For most of us, getting that early sense of achievement creates tremendous confidence and momentum for the rest of the day.

Most people begin their day with emails or some other fairly benign tasks. Then, after a few hours of checking off the less important items from the day's to-do list, they begin to focus on results. This will lead to one of two outcomes: either results are currently strong, and the individual may feel a sense of "Things are going well enough. Maybe I don't have to work so hard today," or results aren't so good, thus creating low confidence and a sense of "No matter what I do, I can't win." Either way, the team loses.

Highly successful people understand the importance of winning the day early. Know what your most important activity is before the day begins, and then get all over it first thing. Win the day early by getting your "1 Must" activity done either first thing each day or as early as possible. Doing so is like a baseball team scoring twenty runs in the first inning. There can be a lot of messing up the rest of the day, and you are still going to win far more days than you will lose.

We would be ripping you off if we didn't manage your expectations on this. Yes, nailing your most important activity daily is the best method of creating flow and controlling your scoreboard; however, **with high-level performance, it is important to know that at times "scoring comes in spurts**." It will probably happen that your team gets focused on nailing the "1 Must" activity but doesn't see immediate results. That's okay. It sometimes happens. Realize, though, that by continuing to be relentless about nailing that most important activity daily, the scoring will happen, and it will tend to come in bunches.

It's like a basketball team running the full-court press. The players can be doing an excellent job running the press for several minutes without seeing any real results from it. The teams that stay with it and continue to relentlessly enforce the press will oftentimes then see a thirty-second period when the other team turns the ball over two or three times, thus allowing them to pick up multiple scoring opportunities.

When a person emphasizes process over results, scoring often comes in spurts. The same principle holds true for teams. The key is to continue believing in and attacking your most important activities early and daily.

SELF-EVALUATION TIME

If you are in a leadership role, answer the following questions with the goal of identifying one thing you can do to improve team cohesion.

1. Could every member of my team clearly state the single most important product goal (a result-oriented goal that the team can achieve within the next twelve months) and the team's vision goal (the result-oriented goal the team wants to achieve in three years or longer)?
2. Do all team members know their daily "3 Most Important" and "1 Must" activities (process goals)?
3. On a scale of 1–10, how good of a job do I think I am doing making sure I have only necessary meetings? Are those meetings run as efficiently as possible? What about conference calls?

If you are not currently in a leadership role, but you are on a team, answer the following questions with the goal of identifying one thing you can do to improve team cohesion.

1. Can I clearly state the single most important product goal (a result-oriented goal that my team can achieve within the next twelve months) and the team's vision goal (the result-oriented goal the team wants to achieve in three years or longer)?
2. Do I know my daily "3 Most Important" and "1 Must" activities (process goals)?
3. On a scale of 1–10, how good of a job do I think I am doing nailing my "1 Must" activity first thing every day?

This chapter began with team cohesion and the 2–1–1 principle, and then it described the flow state and getting your "1 Must" done daily. These concepts might seem separate—one is oriented toward relationships and team building, while the other is more about you fulfilling your own specific role in the best way that you can. In reality, the two topics are closely related. When everyone on a team is in the flow, tackling the priorities, *and* people are pointing at each other for their contributions, a special thing happens: the team itself gets into a flow state. When a team can work together in this optimal way, and a collective flow state emerges, sooner or later, great success will follow.

TEACH IT

For team cohesion it is essential that everyone on the team have clarity around the most important team product goal (result-oriented goal of one year or less), the most important team vision goal (result-oriented goal of three years or more), and each individual's "3 Most Important" and "1 Must" daily goals.

INVERT

(By inverting any fundamental you can learn more)

To slow team cohesion, stop "pointing" and allow interruptions—especially when it is the time to be completing the "1 Must" activity of the day.

"3 MOST IMPORTANT" FOR THE TEAM TO REMEMBER

1. People need not be friends to create highly effective team cohesion. What is necessary is goal commonality and role integrity.
2. *Point* (recognizing a teammate's teamwork-contributing behavior) and *flow* (uninterrupted performance) are two very effective methods of motivating team members to execute on role integrity.
3. A person doesn't need to wear the same jersey as you to be on your team. Clients, prospects, and vendors can become your teammates as well. Using the 2–1–1 (give two compliments, teach one thing, coach one thing) method of communicating is a very effective way to create cohesive relationships.

"1 MUST" TAKEAWAY FOR TEAMS

The single most important thing that any member of a team can do to contribute to the cohesion of the team is to identify and nail daily their "1 Must" activity.

Chapter 5

IT'S OKAY TO DISAGREE: JUST DON'T BE DISAGREEABLE

Disagreeing agreeably: Having as much respect for an alternate opinion as you would for you own

Let's take care of one misconception right here.

The best teams you've ever seen—either in business or in sports—don't agree on everything. They don't think with one mind, or believe in all of the same causes. They're not all friends, and they don't all go home together for barbecues and card games.

And, believe it or not, the diversity is one of the major factors in teams achieving high-level success.

To build a great team, you need people to think differently, and you need different people to fill different roles. **To fully grow, individuals must be challenged with opposing viewpoints and ideas.**

If every person on a team has the same ideas and opinions and the same way of doing things, the team is only as strong as a team of one. For teams to thrive, there must be differing opinions, and that is precisely why it's important to learn how to disagree—agreeably.

It's not us saying it. It's history talking.

General George S. Patton's Third Army became operational in July 1944. Over the next 281 days, it advanced and piled up a record of military accomplishment that may never be equaled. Patton's troops liberated more than 1,500 cities and towns in an area of over 82,000 square miles, killing or wounding half a million German soldiers and capturing almost 1.3 million more. And in doing that, the Third Army lost only 13 casualties for every 100 on the German side.

How did Patton accomplish this? Was it by being a, well, general—ordering people around and demanding obedience from the officers and enlisted men below him?

Absolutely not.

General Patton actually *encouraged* his staff to disagree with him. It didn't matter what rank an officer had. If someone had a problem with one of the strategic decisions being made—and had a valid reason for that opinion—Patton wanted to hear it. If the idea made sense and was a better option, Patton had the self-confidence and a healthy enough ego to take the suggestion and adapt.[1]

Patton wasn't the only one who knew how to disagree agreeably. Prime Minister Winston Churchill of Great Britain was pressuring General George Marshall, the US Army's chief of staff, to send American troops to support the British in North Africa. Marshall called Patton to sound him out on that possibility, and Patton famously took the call in front of his staff.

Marshall suggested that Patton should get ready to take his men to Africa. Patton responded that it would take a minimum of six weeks to train his men to be ready for the heat of the desert—and if that six-week window wasn't observed, the Americans would lose more men to the conditions than to the Germans.

General Marshall listened to General Patton's reasoning, then returned to Churchill and informed him that he would have to wait for American reinforcements. After the proper training period, Patton's Western Task Force eventually landed in Morocco. It destroyed the resistance there—retaking Casablanca and liberating Morocco from German control.

General Patton was open to his team disagreeing with him, and he had the strength and willingness to disagree with General Marshall—but do it in an agreeable way. Patton had the facts to back up his position, and he stood up for his beliefs. Marshall listened with an open mind, gathered the facts, and trusted his frontline person who was close to the action.

By agreeably disagreeing—and eventually coming to an agreement—the two generals saved tens of thousands of troops from being needlessly wounded or killed, setting the stage for the Allies to win World War II.

The ability to have as much respect for a reasoned alternate opinion as you do for your own is a precious skill—and one we're going to help you develop in this chapter.

It couldn't come at a better time, either. The way we communicate now—from "formal" office communication to more casual outlets like Twitter and Facebook—has radically changed in the past decade. There's more literal and figurative space between people, even when they're working on the same team.

When you communicate by email or any other digital method, you have more than just the physical distance between you and the other party. Because you aren't face-to-face, you have the opportunity to use words you might not otherwise use. You can miss some nonverbal cues that just don't exist in cyberspace.

More than ever, there's a huge opportunity for us to get things wrong in how we communicate. We build barriers and enemies when we could be constructively disagreeing. Disagreeing agreeably is a kind of friction that is at the heart of every great organization.

ENCOURAGING DISAGREEMENT

One of the biggest mistakes happening in business right now is that people do not understand the value of disagreeing agreeably; most people don't even know how to do it. Being disagreeable in an agreeable manner promotes alternate and oftentimes improved ways of thinking.

When differing opinions are present, the synergy of intelligence can be released. But only if people disagree agreeably.

Think about it. When was the last time you said—or heard someone on your team say—these words: "Not only is it acceptable to disagree on this team, but it is actually encouraged." Instead, most people are so concerned with being right that the possibility of a better way doesn't cross their minds.

Every person on the planet has fallen prey to this way of thinking at one time or another. Certainly some experience it more than others—but the point is that it is totally normal to confuse our own opinions with fact.

THE MIKE SHANNAHAN RULE

When Tom worked at American Funds, whose parent company is the Capital Group, there was a long-standing rule. It is still known to this day as the "Mike Shannahan Rule," after former chairman Mike Shannahan. At a time when Mike was cycling through meetings with dozens of people throughout the course of a day, he had one iron-clad rule about presenting a dissenting opinion: you were encouraged to give an opposing viewpoint, but if you were going to say something negative or counter to something from somebody else on the team, you had to do it when all of the parties involved were present.

This rule forced everyone to be accountable face-to-face—and it promoted a culture where disagreeing was encouraged, as long as the goals were growth and improvement, and the disagreement was respectful. This is one of the reasons the Capital Group has had such great success. A spirit of fairness and respect is ingrained throughout the organization.

This area of communication is one of the biggest challenges facing modern organizations. Because so much business is done remotely, people lack experience interacting with others in person. Many people come into the business world never having *learned* the skills of being agreeable in the first place. They're never taught how to have constructive conflict in college, and they're usually not rewarded for it at the lower levels of most organizations.

And good old-fashioned office politics are still the same as they ever were. It's very easy—in fact it's common—for people on the same team to disagree with each other about something and take it with them out of the room—only to immediately go find a coworker and complain behind the other person's back.

Corporate America hasn't done much to alleviate this problem, either. In fact, the pressure pushes us in the opposite direction. Most people are trying so hard to be right—to look good to the leaders of the organization—that they aren't in a position to naturally be receptive to others' ideas. To compound matters, with all the platforms we have available online, being disagreeable is way easier than it used to be. Anybody can fire off an angry email or pop off on Twitter about something. The nasty Facebook post is becoming the rule—not the exception.

It is always easier to tear down than it is to build up. Often what has taken years to construct, whether in a friendship or in a business relationship, can be destroyed with words in seconds. Words can be very powerful, especially within the framework of a team.

Three good questions to ask yourself:

1. On a scale of 1–10, how good am I at building others up?
2. On a scale of 1–10, how good am I at tearing others down?
3. Do I put more energy into making myself feel important, or into making others feel important?

OPINIONS ARE DIFFERENT FROM FACTS

To put all this in some perspective, think about what Ben Franklin had to say about it. He was one of the smartest, most influential people in American history. When a colleague brought to his attention that he was becoming impossible to be around because he knew so much that no one could tell him anything, Franklin was wise enough to realize that this mentality was a problem. Not only would it slow his learning, but it would also cause him to end up friendless.

Franklin immediately resolved to change his language. No longer would he allow himself to use words like "certainly" or "undoubtedly"; he would replace them with "I conceive" and "I imagine." When a contradictory opinion was presented, Franklin "denied himself the pleasure of contradicting," and instead forced himself to search for the intellect in the opposing statement.

To Franklin's delight, he found that his conversations with others became much more pleasant, and surprisingly, his friends and colleagues became much more open to his opinions. They were more willing to forgive his mistakes and happier to celebrate his successes.[2]

There is an old saying: "Would you rather be right or would you rather be happy?" Not that we are encouraging anyone to be wrong—that's not the point. The point is, you are going to be wrong, and that's okay. It's much better to be open-minded to the idea that you could be wrong than to become married to any one opinion.

Learning to use these phrases will open the lines of communication and increase the chances of disagreeing agreeably:

"In my opinion . . ."

"Here is what I believe . . ."

"I certainly could be wrong on this, but this is what I think . . ."

Reminding yourself that your opinions are just that, opinions, and not necessarily facts, actually opens the mind up for learning at every curve. Like Benjamin Franklin, you might surprise yourself by realizing just how much other people actually know.

By passionately defending *all* of your ideas, and being willing to fight it out disagreeably with the people around you, just to prove you are right, you're digging yourself into a hole that is difficult to get out of.

It's a common trap, too.

All of us have experienced the "narrowing of the mind" that comes with advancing or defending a position. Part of it comes from how we're wired. As we've talked about repeatedly, the mind can fully focus only on one concept at a time. When you become passionate about something—and you've invested a tremendous amount of time and effort in it—it's easy to get consumed by it. It takes great self-confidence to think that somebody else might have something better or different to contribute. The other part is pure ego. It feels good to be right, and our subconscious minds work hard at getting us to do stuff we think will make people like and respect us more.

The best learners (and best teachers) have discovered that being open to other ideas is so much more productive and attractive than being an absolute authority that they wouldn't want to live any other way. Think about it, nobody likes a know-it-all. **Greatness lies in incorporating the good ideas that come from a variety of sources.**

When you hear great leaders speak within a team setting, you'll quickly find a pattern to that communication. They stay away from absolutes and instead use a lot of collaborative terms that open the lines of communication.

One sure way to do this? Ask for other opinions every time you state your own.

It's something we've learned about personally during the time we've worked together. A few years ago, we were working on a project related to researching the causes of habit formation. We wanted to integrate what we'd learned on the ground in the worlds of sports and business with what had appeared in the research.

After many weeks of Tom picking Jason's brain on the topic of habit formation, it finally occurred to Jason that he should ask Tom what he knew about the subject. Tom laid out his experience and thoughts on the topic for Jason, and Jason immediately knew that he should have asked much sooner. Today they both are still teaching clients Tom's leading-edge model of habit formation.

Here was how the conversation went after Jason realized his mistake. "I know better than thinking I know it all. I'm sorry it took so long for me to figure out that I was supposed to ask you what you knew about habit formation."

Tom's overly gracious response: "Don't worry about it. Don't let that perfectionist mentality get ahold of you. Nobody knows it all. Quit being so hard on yourself."

Jason did not offer excuses in regard to his close-mindedness, and Tom was gracious in understanding. Because both were "agreeable," the experience is just another example of why they work so well together.

OPEN-MINDED LEADERSHIP

The Golden State Warriors get lots of attention because of the stars on their roster—Steph Curry, Kevin Durant, Draymond Green—but coach Steve Kerr has been instrumental in getting all of that star power to merge seamlessly. Kerr has proven over the past several years to be one of the greatest coaches in all of sports (Coach Kerr graciously agreed to allow us to use, for marketing, photos of himself holding up a copy of our last book, so we may be a bit biased on this).

Nonetheless, Kerr has developed a reputation for being beloved by players and others in the organization, and one of the reasons is that he includes everybody in the process. He doesn't lay his authority on people heavily.

In a *Sports Illustrated* story, Chris Ballard described one of Coach Kerr's practices: regularly, he would ask for input from various players about better ways to run certain plays. Kerr had learned this method from his experience as a player under Gregg Popovich of the San Antonio Spurs—who is widely considered to have been the best coach in the NBA over the past decade. One time, when Popovich was drawing up a play at the end of a game, he was determined that a certain player should move over a screen at the top of the key. (If you don't know the terminology, all you need to know is that it involved a very specific defensive move on a certain part of the basketball court.) One of the players in the huddle smacked his hand on the floor and said he should be going under the screen. Because he recognized that the players had a better sense for the speed of the play that would be unfolding on the floor, Popovich went with the player's intuition, and the team ran the play with great success.[3]

The process of being so inclusive serves two purposes—it gives players a voice, and it reminds them that they need to be ready when the questions come. "It keeps me on my toes," said one of the team members, Andre Iguodala. "If he asks, I have to know what I'm talking about. I can't just throw anything out there."

When Kerr consults with various members of the team, or even staff in the front office, they feel like they're contributing to the cause of winning—but more importantly, they feel good about being valued.

That reinforces one of the most basic elements of relationship management. People don't remember what you do as much as they remember how you make them feel.

TRUST AND RESPECT

Even when people on the team can't put their finger on what makes them feel good, they know those feelings when they have them.

Trust and respect are a big part of that stew, and the main ingredient is being open-minded in disagreements. Without trust and respect, people become emotional when disagreements occur. The more emotional a person is, the less the brain works. It's like a see-saw: when emotion goes up, brain power goes down. And as emotion increases, so, too, does disagreeableness.

If you're a team leader, by providing a bedrock support system of trust, respect, and openness, you're giving the people on the team the security to devote all of their attention to their work. They can find solutions to problems, create better ways to do things, and get their jobs done instead of peeling off energy worrying, getting angry, or trying to sort out mixed signals.

Recall the "hierarchy of relationships" that we discussed in Chapter 2. Where do you think the Golden State Warriors players stand on this hierarchy when it comes to their relationship with Steve Kerr?

DEPENDENCE
LOYALTY
TRUST
CREDIBILITY
SUSPICION
FEAR

DEPENDENCE: Do not want to be without the relationship
LOYALTY: A relationship of value is formed
TRUST: Belief that the relationship will bring value
CREDIBILITY: Hope that the relationship may bring value
SUSPICION: Concern that the relationship may cause harm
FEAR: Belief that the relationship will cause harm

The higher up the trust scale, the more likely it is that people will keep negative emotions out of disagreements. When relationships are based on fear and suspicion, it is extremely difficult for people to be agreeable. The closer to credibility and trust relationships are, the more respect will be present, and individuals will naturally be more inclined to be agreeable.

Let's quickly review some of the principles about how trust is developed from Chapter 2:

1. **Endorsement:** When a person has developed trust and respect with others, it paves the way for earning trust and respect in future relationships.
2. **Value:** Make it a point to consistently contribute to the betterment of relationships and the team.
3. **Honesty:** Be honest with people, even when it's difficult and you know the truth will be hard to hear.
4. **Time:** Respect other people's time by, first and foremost, being on time for meetings and appointments. If something

comes up and being on time isn't possible, make a quick call or send a text before arriving late.

5. **Delivery:** If you make a commitment or a promise, it is your obligation to deliver on it.

6. **Ultimate Accountability:** If you come up short on a commitment, do not make an excuse, even if it's a viable excuse. People love to hear these words if you come up short: "I'm sorry, there is no excuse. I will work on this never happening again." People hate to hear your excuses.

When coaches and leaders rule with fear or intentionally create dissension to retain power, they never move from those first two levels of the relationship, fear and suspicion. If you have strong performers on your team, you might be able to survive in the short term with those styles, but they aren't a recipe for long-term success.

Even Steve Jobs was forced to change from running Apple as a dictatorship to a style that placed more value on collaboration among team members up and down the organizational chart.

Why do styles of leadership based on fear and suspicion fail? It's because running a team that way shows the members of the team that only a few specific ways of communication management and relationship development are supported in the organization.

If you're an autocratic tyrant, you're going to have a team of people who know how to respond only to an autocratic tyrant. Sure, they might be united against you, but you're kidding yourself if you think you'll be able to develop team members with loyalty when all they hear are orders and threats.

How the relationship between leaders and team members is developed and maintained also dictates how relationships *between* team members work. If you have a culture of fear and suspicion on your team and it's coming straight from the top, disagreements are going to be handled with fear and suspicion.

You can guess how likely it is for those to be resolved agreeably.

BECOMING AGREEABLE

It is immensely valuable to understand what happens in teams when people disagree without being agreeable. When an employee is disagreeable with the boss, the employee is usually thinking:

- This person shouldn't be leading.
- Our team won't win with this leadership.
- By speaking up, I'm going to be fired.

Conversely, when the boss is aware that an employee doesn't agree, the boss is often thinking:

- This person is disrespectful.
- We can't win with players like this.
- Am I losing control?

Disagreeing should not be viewed as arguing. Arguments are fueled by the goal of "winning." But you can't win an argument. You can't because if you lose it, you lose it; and if you win it, you lose it.

Why?

Because even if you "win" and shoot the other person's argument full of holes, you haven't "converted" that person. You have made him or her feel inferior and resentful. Many times, you will have made an enemy.

Your goal should be to pull value out of multiple—and often disagreeing—opinions.

Each time, ask yourself these three questions:

1. What is the most valuable piece of information in the opposing opinion?
2. Is there a way to combine the value from the opposing opinion with the value from my opinion?
3. If I can't use this information now, is there another place for it—either to solve another problem or to save it for a problem I anticipate having in the future?

With this strategy, almost *nothing* gets wasted. Even the pieces that don't end up being useful for the current problem are banked to use another day.

Like most skills, being agreeable is something that can be taught. You can decide that it's important, make it a core value in your organization, and teach it to your teams.

WHEN WERE YOU EVER TAUGHT
TO DISAGREE AGREEABLY?

We can't stress this point enough. **You *want* people on your team to disagree.** You want them to bring different ideas, and you want those ideas to be able to compete for prime space. If the team always thinks alike, it will only ever be as good as the single idea it generates.

You aren't giving yourself the best odds.

To create a spirit of agreeable disagreement, leaders need to set clear ground rules for how the process will play out. Team members need to know that if they put in a good-faith effort and have support for what they say, they're welcome to be heard at any time.

But being heard is just one piece. The team needs to be in a place where it can be open to what it's hearing. You need to create a culture of appreciation for new and different ideas.

We've had great success with a simple slate of ground rules that remind team members of their basic responsibilities:

1. **Withhold Judgment and Listen with an Open Mind**

   It's easy to scoff at an unfamiliar idea and say it will never work. There's comfort in doing what you've always done. But if you trust that the team has been assembled properly (which, granted, is a big "if"), you have to be willing to let a team member's idea play out before you critique and criticize. The key here is to *never* interrupt. Stephen Covey said it well when he said, "Seek first to understand, then to be understood."[4]

2. **Respect Others' Ideas as Much as You Do Your Own**

   We find that simply reminding team members that their colleagues also have brains—and that they themselves could be wrong—is a simple way to keep people engaged and listening to new ideas. If you can remove some of the stigma from being "wrong" during the idea generation phase, you're making the atmosphere more conducive to producing good ideas. If people are afraid to speak up because they'll be ridiculed, or held responsible if an idea ultimately isn't successful (rather than because of something they did or didn't do), you will never get their greatest ideas. Remember this very famous saying from Coach John Wooden: "It's what you learn after you know it all that counts."

3. Always Begin with the Positive

Listen thoroughly to another person with a spirit of trying to understand what he or she has to say before explaining your point. After listening to the idea in full, always start your comments with what you like about their idea. Ask yourself what the necessary conditions are for this idea to work. If you could execute it, what would be its greatest benefit? Most people in this situation tend to ask what the risks are and why the idea won't work. Do not do that at this point. The greatest minds operate the opposite way. They listen in the spirit of searching to build up rather than to tear down.

Once you've finished with the "data acquisition" part of the process, you might be in a position to disagree. That's okay, but there's a way to do that productively.

It starts with *everybody* in the room understanding the value of disagreeing. It means that disagreeing isn't a personal attack, and it isn't aggressive. You're not making a judgment about somebody's intelligence or quality of work. The group is coming together to find the best path. And remember, your view is not necessarily fact but much more likely just your *opinion*.

If you do disagree, you have to come from a place of knowledge and gentleness. Saying "I don't like this," or "It will never work that way," aren't great ways to disagree. Always begin with the positive. Start by saying, for example, "What I like about your opinion is . . ." or, "What you are saying makes sense, and I believe that if we figure out the best way to apply it, it could work."

When the San Antonio point guard insisted on Coach Popovich changing the play, he didn't say it had to happen because he wasn't happy about his role, or that there was no way the coach's way could work. He combined the current value of Pop's play with one change in execution.

"THE GREATEST STRENGTH IS GENTLENESS" (ABRAHAM LINCOLN)

Gentleness is a highly underrated part of communicating. So much of our culture rewards the person who talks the loudest or says the most outrageous thing that it has inevitably seeped into our teams.

But what happens when you see an argument start to brew? The people involved get amped up and start tossing facts and insults back and forth, and at the end nobody has learned anything new or seen a different perspective. You just have people in a sweat after yelling for an hour. What happens more often than not in an argument is that it ends with each of the contestants more firmly convinced than ever that he or she is absolutely right.

When you use a gentle, nonthreatening tone, you're reinforcing that you aren't making a judgment about the person with whom you disagree. You're on the same path to finding the best solution.

For years, Tom Bartow served as Coach Wooden's "opening act" during the Coach's speeches for American Funds. Tom would speak to the group for forty-five minutes, then circle around to watch the Coach's talk from the crowd before meeting him in the back and returning to Coach Wooden's condo.

In a few of the talks, Coach Wooden spoke in an unflattering way about General Patton, and some of the supposedly autocratic ways in which he operated. One week, Tom had been reading an article about Patton that examined some of the common misconceptions about the General. The article recounted anecdotes that revealed some of the advanced leadership tactics—and emotional intelligence—we know he had.

One of the stories featured a subject that was near and dear to Coach Wooden's heart: socks.

General Patton was a fanatic about socks. He insisted that his soldiers have the best socks, and that they keep them clean—because an army fights on its feet.

Coach Wooden was equally fanatical about socks and feet. He famously spent his first meeting of the season showing his players how to pay close attention to their socks and shoes to avoid blisters and injuries.

Tom was nervous about approaching Coach Wooden about this. After all, Wooden was getting standing ovations before and after every speech, and at the Final Four in Seattle that year, Bill Gates had requested—and was granted—the seat next to Coach Wooden.

But Tom also remembered two of the central values that Coach Wooden had shared with him over the years: a friend will tell you, in a *gentle* manner, when you're wrong or mistaken.

Tom knew he and Coach Wooden were friends. And he believed it was important to share with the Coach what he had learned—gently. So, one day, Tom asked Coach Wooden how many times he thought he had told the story of putting on socks the correct way.

"Many times," Coach Wooden said.

Tom responded by saying he had run across a story about somebody else who had thought socks were important. He handed Coach Wooden a copy of the article about General Patton and said he thought he would enjoy it.

The Coach trusted and respected Tom, so he read it. And Tom never heard Coach Wooden say anything negative about General Patton again.

Teammates owe it to one another to resolve differences. A great way to gently address a dissenting opinion is to say, "If the roles were reversed, I would want you to talk to me about this." When a disagreement occurs between teammates, get to a solution quickly and gently.

Questions to consider:

1. On a scale of 1–10, how much do I listen with an open mind?
2. When is the last time I said, out loud, "This is my opinion and I could be wrong"?

LEARN TO LISTEN

The foundation of a lot of Tom's teaching comes from the times he spent with Coach John Wooden over the years. Many of the leadership, communication, and dispute resolution strategies Coach Wooden talked about decades ago have come to be supported by research as best practices.

One of Coach Wooden's favorite tactics was to hand out a small laminated card with a picture of an owl sitting on a branch.

On the card was printed one of the Coach's favorite poems (author unknown):

> *A wise old owl sat on an oak.*
> *The more he heard, the less he spoke.*
> *The less he spoke, the more he heard.*
> *Now wasn't he a wise old bird?*

At the very bottom of the card was a quote from the Coach himself written in all caps: "LISTEN IF YOU WANT TO BE HEARD."

That sounds simplistic, but when you really think about it, you realize that communication has only two elements: you can speak, or you can listen.

When it comes to speaking, there are literally limitless training options—books on how to speak, write, promote, act, and do almost anything else to get noticed. But when it comes to listening, the sources of advice are much fewer—and much more abstract.

Answer two questions:

1. When have I ever worked on listening as a skill?
2. When have I ever thoroughly examined the questions I asked?

Listening is 50 percent (or more, if you listen to Coach Wooden) of communication, yet it gets virtually no attention in training circles. If you're speaking, you can't be listening or learning.

1. Ask Open-Ended Questions

You can become a better listener by becoming a better asker. It's hard for most people to put their finger on why they enjoy interviews conducted by certain people, like Oprah Winfrey or Howard Stern. It's because those interviewers do a fantastic job asking thought-provoking, open-ended questions. When you can get somebody to stop and think, the answer is usually going to be productive. Want to see the opposite? Watch most postgame interview scrums at a sporting event. The players and coaches are usually inundated with questions that lend themselves to a one- or two-word answer, or they're given impossibly vague questions that make them do all the work for a lazy interviewer: "On the last play, did you know you were going to score?"

as opposed to "What was the single most important thing you were focused on in that last play?"

2. **Close Your Eyes**

Nonverbal communication is extremely important. There is a large amount of information communicated in the tone, pace, and energy of what is being said. Research on communication states that only 7 percent of communication is what is being said (the actual words), while 93 percent of any message comes from "how" it is said. If you're talking to somebody on the phone, try closing your eyes as you have the conversation. When you do that, you become much more attuned to those other variables. You simply hear a lot more.

3. **Don't Interrupt**

When you interrupt people, you're sending the clear message that you think your opinion is more important than theirs. You're telling those people that you're not interested in learning from them. It's also a symptom of another conversational hazard—thinking about what you're going to say next instead of listening to what the person you're talking to is saying. You're not on a stage performing lines in a play. Listen, allow yourself time to think, and then respond. Grow the conversation. It's not a competition.

These sound like basic, simple rules that are easy to follow. But if you track your own conversations for the next few hours, we'll bet you will be shocked by the results. How many times did you ask non-open-ended questions? How much did you pay attention to tone, pace, and energy? How many times did you interrupt?

When we work with high-level coaching clients, we start them out by asking for a concentrated five minutes for every call they make. For that first five minutes, we ask them to make a full effort to listen and speak with their eyes closed. This eye-closing experience shows our clients how much their listening has been impaired by the distraction of the computer screen. Sitting in front of a computer screen is commonplace in today's workplace. Remember, the mind can fully focus only on one thing at a time, and if you are focused on what is on the computer screen, you cannot be fully invested in listening. This is one of the reasons we have found that listening is under siege.

But after working on listening skills for just a few days, something interesting begins to happen—and we've seen it work for virtually everybody who puts in this effort. **Improving listening skills will, in turn, make you into a much better speaker.**

That's right. By improving how you ask questions and listen, you improve your ability to speak.

You'll start to think about how the message you're about to deliver will be received. The subtext is "If I were the person on the other end of this communication, how would I hear it?" This is the difference between thinking *about* your clients and thinking *like* your clients. At first glance, this may look very difficult to do consistently. It might surprise you to find that if you work on it, it's actually much easier to accomplish than it might at first appear. Working on this skill will certainly enhance open-mindedness and communication.

Does that mean you have to move into a totally passive mode, where you can't make challenging points that need to be made? Absolutely not. But by being an empathic speaker and better listener—even with people you don't particularly like or want to deal with—you're improving your own strategic ability to communicate with them.

You'll be going into every conversation with an open mind—instead of simply trying ram your own points home.

Questions to consider:

1. How well do I know my facts before presenting my ideas?
2. How well do I accept others' ideas when they go against my opinion?
3. Do I comment on the value of opposing opinions before getting into the value of my own opinion?

TEACH IT

Unresolved disagreements are typically a result of a person's ego getting in the way of progress. Disagreements between teammates are the breeding ground for a "cancer" that can bounce a team from "playoff contender" to loser! When in doubt, listen—and then ask these questions:

1. What is the most valuable concept in the opposing opinion?
2. How can I combine the value in the opposing opinion with the value in my opinion to form a stronger new opinion?

INVERT

(By inverting any fundamental you can learn more)

If disagreements are not encouraged, a team becomes one-dimensional and success is significantly decreased.

"3 MOST IMPORTANT" FOR
THE TEAM TO REMEMBER

1. When you interrupt, you are sending a clear message that the opposing opinion doesn't matter to you.
2. Respect others' ideas as much as you do your own: remind yourself often, "I respect this person and know he (or she) has good ideas."
3. When evaluating an opposing opinion, always search for and begin with the positive points of the opposing viewpoint.

"1 MUST" TAKEAWAY FOR TEAMS

Encourage disagreeing opinions and combine the top value points from each to create a more effective approach.

Chapter 6

DEVELOPING THE NO-VICTIM MENTALITY

No-Victim Mentality: The refusal by the team and its members to become powerless

FOR SALE—ONE VICTIM MENTALITY
PRICE—YOURS FOR FREE
COST—A LIFETIME OF MISERY

Any team or organization can have the greatest game plan on earth and the biggest star power players, but if it doesn't also develop the ability to avoid falling into the victim trap, it's going to be one of those vulnerable teams that the best coaches always love competing against. You have to be willing to reject characterizing yourself or the team as a "victim."

Why?

Because life happens to all of us. No team, no organization, experiences life without problems, and generally those problems are significant. Players and teams with a victim mentality allow those problems to become big, obvious, exploitable weaknesses.

The dynasty teams in sports and business aren't flustered in times of adversity. Highly successful teams have learned to work through tough times, satisfying their customers and developing talented and productive team members. **The best teams actually *thrive* in the face of adversity.**

The Ohio State University football program, coached by Urban Meyer, is a perfect example. Coach Meyer and his staff have been relentless in their recruiting efforts, building the strongest offensive and defensive teams filled with players who perfectly align with their strategy. A player's "star" power isn't as important as how well his skills and attitude fit with the plan. And making the team is just the beginning.

That's when the real work begins. Players are consistently drilled on the importance of "above the line" behavior. This approach forces team cohesion on the field that supports the team's desired success. There is no blaming or excuse-making. Having a victim mentality is never allowed. Instead, the emphasis is on complete accountability and relentlessly focusing on solutions.

A player works to his potential and behaves in a manner that promotes team success or the necessary adjustments are made. Players know up front what is expected of them, their expectations are managed effectively, and coaches follow through to uphold the integrity of the team. No matter what the circumstances are, coaches and players alike are trained to focus on what they can control rather than on what they cannot control.

When individuals or teams focus on the things they cannot control, they become, by definition, victims. They have become powerless. Highly successful people and teams have learned that in the face of adversity it's best to focus on the things they can control. They identify those one or two most important activities, and they nail those "controllables" daily.

In 2014, Ohio State won the national championship in a season chock-full of adversity. After losing their first game of the season at home and then having not one, but two starting quarterbacks experience season-ending injuries, the coaching staff and players worked tirelessly not to become victims of circumstance.

The team stayed focused on practicing, playing with "relentless effort," as Coach Meyer put it in his book *Above the Line*. Meyer repeatedly told his team, "We will go four to six seconds, point A to point B, as hard as we can. This is the culture of Ohio State football, it is what we believe, and how we behave. It is who we are."[1]

Giving the team clear optics on the one most important thing they could control (relentless effort—four to six seconds on every play) allowed them to refrain from focusing on all those things they could not control.

The team defied all odds and won fourteen games in a row to finish the season as college football's number one program.

Can you even imagine losing arguably the most important person on your team not once, but twice in the same year? And still refusing to let it stop you from completely dominating the competition?

College football is an intensely competitive field. When things go wrong for those Ohio State teams—say, a star's injury or any other difficulty within the organization—it would be easy and understandable for the people on those teams to say to themselves, well, it just wasn't our year.

Teams with the "no-victim mentality" don't get trapped that way. They refuse to become powerless, and in so doing they set themselves up for consistent growth and success.

In this chapter, we're going to teach you how to establish the no-victim mindset. Once you learn it, you'll be ready for any challenge you face.

PLANTING THE RIGHT SEEDS

The seeds for the strategies we use to establish these characteristics were planted decades ago, when Tom Bartow was in his first life as a basketball coach. His first coaching job was at a small high school north of Kansas City called West Platte.

He wasn't there more than a week before he had heard a dozen times from the faculty and students how the team had never beaten one of its main rivals, Kearney High School. The pattern repeated itself several times as Tom moved to different jobs. At Moberly High School, the devoted followers of the team would talk about how the team could never seem to win at Kirksville High School. Even when Tom made it into the college ranks, the people in the athletic department at the University of Missouri–St. Louis would complain about how hard it was to have to go to Eastern Illinois.

The goal, they said, was just to get out of that rowdy gym without being embarrassed.

The seductive part about every one of those conversations was that it was both *true* and a built-in excuse for continuing to struggle.

West Platte had *never* beaten Kearney. If Tom's team kept losing to Kearney, well, that's what was expected.

That rowdy gym at Eastern Illinois? How was anybody expected to go in there and beat that team in that place? If the team went in and lost by four or five points, it was almost like winning, right?

No, it wasn't.

What Tom and his teams were being offered in each of those scenarios was to continue to be a victim. To continue to be the easy prey for the other teams, who were having their own conversations about how great it was going to be to face West Platte,

Moberly, or UM–St. Louis, because those guys always came in and rolled over.

It's free and easy to become a victim, and for a lot of people, it even feels good. It feels like the responsibility for failing has come off your shoulders, and it isn't your fault. Somebody else was better or stronger, or there was some excuse that just made it *impossible* for you to do well.

But if you buy into that victim mentality, you quickly become powerless. You're no longer steering your own course. You're just a raft without oars, going where the current takes you.

Tom refused to accept that, and as a result, he started becoming known as a coach who turned losing programs around. His second-year record as a high school coach was 43–7, with teams that had been perennial losers. As a college coach, he took a team that had been 9–17 the previous year to a 17–9 record the next season and a ranking in the top thirty teams nationally.

People think that the strategies coaches like Urban Meyer or Tom Bartow use are way more sophisticated. The opposite is true.

The best coaches use the simplest approaches—the ones that stay the closest to the psychological principles that underpin all of us as humans. They understand what makes us tick, and they build simple systems to exploit what we're already wired to do.

It works just as well for a high school basketball program as it does at a high-powered corporate team looking for another stellar year.

Tom's approach was the same at every stop in his coaching career—and also throughout his time in the corporate world after he transitioned from basketball. When he recognized the victim mentality, he focused on one thing for the team to attack. He gave them one big, aggressive (but attainable) skill to master, and set about making the team feel more in control of its destiny.

At West Platte, the "one thing" was precise passing. At Moberly, it was run, run, run. At UM–St. Louis, it was knees bent.

You can predict what happened.

West Platte beat Kearney.

Moberly beat Kirksville.

UM–St. Louis made a late comeback to beat Eastern Illinois—in their gym.

All of those victories happened in Tom's first year with those teams.

The victories certainly make this story more fun to tell, but winning the big game isn't even necessary to understand why this is important. Because you're not always going to win the big game. Nobody does.

High-level success is not about controlling everything. It's about realizing you can always control *something*. Finding something to control makes winning *more likely*, because the team is prepared to *deal* with adversity. The real secret is learning to *thrive* on adversity, and this occurs when teams control the most important "one thing."

ESCAPE FROM THE BOX

Basketball games, football games—and all sporting events, for that matter—are just entertainment. Let's take this study to a more meaningful level. Colonel Ed Hubbard's plane was shot down over North Vietnam in July 1966. The US Air Force navigator, who at the time held the rank of first lieutenant, ejected, landed, and successfully evaded capture for eight hours. The North Vietnamese eventually captured Ed, and he spent nearly seven years as a prisoner of war. His cell was roughly six by six feet.

Ed's restroom facility was a small bucket. He was beaten and tortured almost every day during his captivity. If anyone should be allowed to have a victim mentality, it should be Ed and his fellow POWs. In his book *Escape from the Box*, Ed wrote, "The single most important lesson we learned in prison was that fear is nothing more than a feeling that comes over you when you lack confidence in your ability to cope with life as it has been dealt to you. Once you step up and accept full responsibility for your own future and your own fate, and once you step up and find out how simple it is to cope with life, fear is not such a big deal anymore."

A fellow prisoner once remarked to Ed, "This is the most expensive education you are ever going to receive in your life." They survived because in the harshest of conditions, they refused to be victims.[2]

Colonel Hubbard recently told Tom that he made the decision fifty years ago last Christmas to never have a victim mentality, and he has literally not had one bad day since. He says it is also the reason he will never have posttraumatic stress disorder (PTSD). There are no laws or rules requiring anyone to have a bad day: it is a conscious decision each one of us makes. As Holocaust survivor Viktor Frankl said it this way in *Man's Search for Meaning*, after coming out of Auschwitz: "In the concentration camp every circumstance conspires to make the prisoner lose his hold. All the familiar goals in life are taken away. What alone remains is the ability to choose one's attitude in a given set of circumstances."[3]

THE VICTIM MENTALITY

To fully develop the no-victim mentality, it is important to realize first what a victim mentality is. Here are the stages of the victim mentality:

1. **Failure to Recognize:** Unfortunately, recognizing the victim mentality is harder than it sounds. It's difficult to recognize because of our biological tendency to focus on problems (recall PCT, for problem-centric thought). It is extremely common for people to feel powerless at times because of their circumstances. The first step to not being a victim is to realize when you are headed down the victim path. The good news is that we all have a built-in alarm system that is 100 percent effective at letting us know when we are moving in the wrong direction. The alarm is negative emotion. As humans, we do not possess the ability to feel sad, angry, scared, stressed, or anxious unless our mind is focused on a problem. Anytime a person experiences a negative emotion, it is a signal that he or she has just started down the path toward becoming a victim. This is where you must learn to recognize what's happening and take control.

2. **Succumb and Wallow in It:** If a person fails to recognize that he or she is becoming a victim, the natural progression is to accept it and succumb. Once a person succumbs to the victim mentality, however, that person has become powerless. The circumstance or problem is now in control, and the person just along for the ride. Unfortunately, this stage can last for an extended period of time—for some people, it can be an entire lifetime. Some people in an organization, without knowing it, can actually become salespeople for adopting a victim mentality. They speak only of the difficulties and dangers without offering solutions. Therein lies the danger of the victim mentality—failure to recognize it creates ideal conditions for it to spread.

3. **Spread It:** It's true that when a person experiences the

victim mentality, a subconscious cry for help is to discuss it with others. Gerry Spence, one of the top attorneys in the country, wrote, "Words kill and words maim."[4] When a victim starts describing what he or she is going through to a fellow team member, that person is in effect telling his or her teammates that they might also get the same "disease." When people at the management level, in discussing a situation, fail to offer possible solutions to a problem, or to explore ways to take advantage of what is happening, they are also spreading the disease. Unfortunately, **discussing problems with others (without offering solutions) is like purposely spreading the flu bug**. Talking to others about problems increases the likelihood of the other people getting pulled into the PCT trap. This is how the victim-mentality epidemic spreads in organizations.

BE AWARE OF THE DANGERS OF THE VICTIM MENTALITY

The victim mentality, like any disease, tends to follow a certain path.

1. IT FREEZES—It causes inaction. The mind will always be quick to go to the dark side. Allowing yourself to feel like a victim will paralyze action.
2. IT'S EXTREMELY CONTAGIOUS—When one person succumbs to the victim mentality, he or she will want to spread it to others. The flu contagion is nothing compared to the victim mentality.
3. REGRESSION IS THE NORM—Positive action is paralyzed and it becomes acceptable to go backward.

Ask yourself a couple of very difficult questions about your team:

1. What has the team become a victim to?
2. Who is selling the victim mentality to the team?

DEVELOPING THE NO-VICTIM MENTALITY

The ramifications of falling into the victim trap go beyond just a poorly functioning team. As we have already stated, this negative mentality works a lot like the flu virus, in that if you get a victim in close proximity to others, the mentality spreads.

Why?

Because people who feel powerless often lash out in fear or anger. They want to talk about how they feel, because talking about it is one of the few things they feel like they still have the freedom and control to do.

It sounds nice to be able to confide in a friend or a colleague about your struggles, and we're certainly not suggesting that the folks on your teams not be friendly and supportive. But **when people on teams talk within the framework of being powerless and turn into victims, they run the very high risk of infecting other players and teams with the same thoughts**. Pretty soon, folks on the other teams are getting discouraged about problems they hadn't even considered previously—real or imaginary.

You can see it clearly on a poorly functioning NFL team. When the quarterback starts taking some hits and blames his offensive line when talking to the media, the other players in the locker room certainly notice. They usually respond by letting the quarterback get pounded even more—something that directly hurts the team's chances to win. The feeling? We don't have a chance to win, so what's the difference?

Then, after the season is over, when it comes time to evaluate players, the responses are almost always some version of the same answer. It was a hopeless situation. What did you expect?

The victim mentality morphs from one person's problem to a cancer in the clubhouse. In his first book, *10-Minute Toughness*, Jason wrote, "Excuses promote underachieving." Excuses, for the most part, are an individual thing. Think of it this way: when someone makes excuses on your team, it's like one person having the flu. **A victim mentality is like having everyone on the team with the flu.**

The victim mentality is contagious in a very bad way, and in many cases will require a relentless search for solutions. Once a team succumbs to the victim mentality, their chances of ever reaching their potential are drastically reduced.

It is much easier to help one person overcome a victim mentality than it is to move seven, twelve, or fifty team members. On a team, there are many minds to shift. All minds do not shift or move at once or at the same rate of speed, making the issue even more dynamic.

If, as a leader, you sense that victimhood taking hold in your team, the next step needs to be immediate, and you need to pursue it relentlessly. You must identify the single place where you believe you can establish a competitive advantage in the face of that adversity. It is essential to identify one important thing you can control, and then you must attack it.

To avoid becoming a victim, you must always have a solution on the board. Expectancy theory says that what you think about expands. It describes what happens to most people when they're confronted with a problem. When the problem occupies your thoughts, it becomes larger—often to the point where it consumes you. The key process we're trying to take control over here is what happens when you identify that negative emotion and the problem that goes with it. Instead of focusing on the negative emotion and the problem itself, direct your attention to the solution—the action that will improve the problem. **Identify just one thing that you and your team can attack, and instantly the victim mentality vanishes.**

In 2006, two years before the economic downturn would force General Motors and Chrysler into government bailouts, Ford decided to take advantage of the great credit markets to take a huge loan. They used the loan to restructure and streamline their business so it could focus on smaller, more fuel-efficient cars—and be ready if something were to disrupt the automotive market.

Of course, two years later it happened. The automakers saw sales declines of 20 and 25 percent year over year. GM and Chrysler had to reorganize through bankruptcy and government cash. But even though Ford suffered huge losses, it didn't require any government intervention. Even through the downturn, they were able to continue their singular focus on producing a line of small, efficient cars that could compete with Japanese and German models.

That foresight and refusal to play the victim to the marketplace that almost destroyed two huge competitors helped Ford increase its stock price from around $1 in 2008 to more than $18 in 2011.

To develop the no-victim mentality, follow these steps:

1. **Get Your Mind Right:** When bad things happen, don't allow yourself to think, "Poor me, this is just my luck." This is where you must adopt the mindset that you *never* again have to be powerless. Ted Jones (former managing partner of Edward Jones) used to repeatedly say, "Even when the rules change, there is *always* something you can take advantage of." Ted was right. No matter what the circumstance or problem, we as humans always have the ability to im-

prove the situation. It may be true that the circumstance or the problem may not be malleable; however, we know that, at the bare minimum, we can always change for the better how we are dealing with the problem. **Never again allow yourself to say, think, or believe the words "There is nothing I can do about it."** There is always something you can do about it. Even if it's just a small improvement on how you are dealing with the problem, you can always make it better. Even an inch of progress over time crosses the widest expanse.

2. **Recognize It:** Anytime you experience stress, anxiety, fear, anger, or depression, it means your thoughts are focused on a problem or negative situation. Realize that your mind can fully focus only on one thing at a time. If you are focused on a problem, you cannot be focused on the power you have to do something about it. It all begins with negative emotion. When you experience any negative emotion, that must be your cue that you are heading in the direction of allowing yourself to become a victim to circumstance. Negative emotion is the alarm that tells you to say, in your head, "I know what's going on here. My mind is trying to convince me that I don't have power. Not me, no way. I can always improve my situation, always!"

3. **Pick One Thing and Attack:** The key here is to do it quickly and relentlessly. Once you realize that the victim-mentality winds are beginning to blow, you must immediately identify the one thing you are going to do to take advantage of the circumstance instead of moaning over it. This no-victim mentality is for teams what the Relentless Solution Focus, or RSF, is for individuals—a concept we wrote about in *Organize Tomorrow Today*. With the no-victim mentality, the faster you are at picking one thing for your team to attack,

the better. The longer it takes to attack, the more likely it is that the victim mentality will begin to spread. You can be certain that on teams, if one person is falling prey to the victim mentality, it is quite likely that others soon will be falling to it as well. Stop it dead in its tracks, do it quickly, and be relentless about attacking.

MASTERING IT

Sergio García is a great illustration of this transformation. García first got attention for his golf game when he was in his first year as a pro, in 1999. He was paired with Tiger Woods in the final round of the PGA Championship, and he gave the best player in the world a run for his money before eventually finishing second.

García spent most of the next decade being considered one of the next big things in golf—always on the verge of winning his first major championship. But he struggled when holding the lead in the final round, and he lost some notable tournaments.

The most famous setback might have been at the 2007 British Open, when García went to a playoff with Pádraig Harrington after the two tied through seventy-two holes. García's shot on an extremely hard par-3 was almost perfectly struck, but the ball hit the flag and bounced off the green. He made a bogey and ended up losing the playoff. In his press conference afterward, García said luck was conspiring against him; he thought he might never win a major, because he was playing against more than just the rest of the field.

It was a classic example of a victim mentality—rendering yourself powerless to affect your own outcome.

García would struggle for another few years before gaining some perspective and self-confidence in his late thirties. He said his performance in majors wouldn't define him, and giving his best effort was all he could do. At the 2017 Masters, he made an eagle on the fifteenth hole to tie for the lead. He would go on to beat Justin Rose in a playoff to earn his first major. García stopped playing the victim role, and he immediately became the Masters champion.

We have all heard the phrase "The grass is always greener on the other side." Many of us believe the forces of the world are working against us. There is a word for this type of thinking: "paranoia." Our problem-centric tendency causes us to believe there is more negative than good in the world; however, in reality, so many more good things happen than bad. The inverse of paranoia is believing that the forces of the world are conspiring in our favor. When negative things happen, "inverse paranoids" believe that they're happening for a reason, and that in the end the negative experience will help propel something positive in some way.

Such was obviously the case with Sergio García.

CASE STUDY—THE DOL RULING

The biggest sports moments often give us great, obvious examples of the principles we're discussing, but the victim mentality can leak into a team setting in business in a much more subtle way. As a leader, if you aren't prepared to see it and confront it, the problem becomes much larger and harder to resolve down the road.

One of the reasons the problem is so pervasive is directly related to it being hard to spot.

As stated above, we're all wired to be focused on problems. If your body tells you you're hungry, you're going to be distracted until you solve that problem. If you feel powerless, your natural response is to feel discouraged and overwhelmed and then give up. The goal, then, is to intervene before this feeling of powerlessness entrenches.

As a team leader or team member, someday someone will try to sell you a membership on the team of victims. It's easy to buy in, and once you accept membership, you are basically saying, "When things become difficult, I will quit." Ironically, being on a team can sometimes make an individual feel powerless—especially if you're lower on the totem pole than most. If decisions are being made above you, and it feels like everything on your plate is being dictated to you without any consideration for your skills or interests, it's certainly easy to see how you might head toward that victim mentality.

But whether we're talking about that kind of situation or one where the players are more equal in rank, the first step you need to take is to get your mind right. When Tom started with Edward Jones, Ted Jones himself was one of his mentors. And one of the things that came out of Ted's mouth most often was something anybody who knew him could have quoted: "Even when the rules change, there is *always* something you can take advantage of."

Just like we're wired to focus on problems, as humans we are also incredibly adaptable—as long as we put our minds to it. You can improve any situation you're in, as long as you have the right mindset.

But wait. We can already hear what you're saying next.

Some circumstances truly are beyond your power to change. You really don't have control.

That's 100 percent true.

But what you do have control over is how you deal with a situation or a problem. So even if you're facing a truly intractable issue with people on your team, or others outside your building whom you know won't bend, you can choose to set your mind to improving in terms of how you *respond* to what's in front of you.

The best people learn to adapt, and to go over, under, or around.

If a team (or its leader) doesn't notice this pervasive feeling of powerlessness in time, the team will almost certainly fall into the victim trap and take its hands off the steering wheel, so to speak. And this isn't a temporary situation. **Plenty of individuals go an entire lifetime in a state of victimhood.**

The only thing that stops the spiral is for the problem to peter out on its own—or for a leader to step in and take control.

Here's an example. In July 2015, a very successful financial advisor said to Tom, "Have you heard about this upcoming Department of Labor ruling? It's going to change our business for the worse."

For the next eighteen months, financial advisors across the country were being pulled into the victim mentality concerning the DOL ruling that would change fiduciary responsibilities with all retirement accounts. In essence, the ruling meant that countless hours would need to be spent with clients explaining the official changes, as well as repapering those accounts.

Most financial advisors chose to allow their minds to focus on the additional "countless hours" of work. However, the most successful advisors realized that "when the rules change, there is *always* something you can take advantage of." They recognized the potential for falling prey to the victim mentality and instead chose to identify one thing they could do to take advantage of the situation.

Tom and Jason were quick to recognize the problem and swiftly pointed out that the DOL ruling was a fantastic opportunity to deepen relationships with current clients, as well as a great way to bring in new clients. Tom crafted a presentation that efficiently outlined the ruling and why it was a good thing for clients. Jason pushed advisors to "attack the one thing" by presenting the information to at least three current clients, prospects, or centers of influence daily.

Many advisors, because of the DOL ruling, fell prey to the victim mentality. Those who did experienced downturns in business in 2016 of 10 to 20 percent. However, those who chose to attack were fortunate: they saw positive gains in their year-over-year production.

All of us have draining and stressful interactions with the same people week in and week out, or month in and month out. It could be a supervisor, a competitor, a peer, or even a family member. Because of the consistently negative nature of the interaction, it can be very easy to give in to the victim mentality. No matter what I do, I can't win with them. Never give in to losing, never. Remember, **there is always something you can do to make it better**.

By creating a system for handling those situations, you're mentally preparing yourself for what's coming—and reducing some of that negativity and stress. For example, if you always have a tense conversation with your team leader about the results of a weekly report, you can resolve to come into that meeting each week with one new business idea to reframe the conversation. Or you could make it a competition for yourself to find one thing in the interaction that you do agree with, or that you could learn from.

Just as it's a leader's responsibility to sniff out the warning smoke of a team falling into the victim trap, it's your responsibility to identify it in yourself. This is another prime example of channel capacity at work: you can't be truly focused on more than one thing at a time, and if you're consumed by a problem or a feeling of helplessness, you can't be focused on a solution.

By definition, that means you're falling into the victim trap.

Let's be clear: this is definitely not an easy thing to do. However, when an individual escapes from victimhood, his or her confidence level, degree of self-reliance, and sense of inner power increase dramatically. When your team adopts the no-victim mentality, the collective mindset becomes solution focused, new-comers to the team become vaccinated quickly, and the team begins to consistently win at a higher level. Once a team has developed a no-victim mentality, it has laid the final stage of the groundwork it needed to move to the dynasty level.

TEACH IT

Teach one person that the first key to developing the no-victim mentality is to realize there is *always* something you can do to improve your situation . . . ALWAYS.

INVERT

(By inverting any fundamental you can learn more)

If you don't develop the no-victim mentality, you will always be powerless in the face of adversity.

"3 MOST IMPORTANT" FOR THE TEAM TO REMEMBER

Three Steps to Developing the No-Victim Mentality:

1. **Get Your Mind Right:** The world is not working against you, the grass isn't greener on the other side, and you can always make your situation better . . . always.
2. **Recognize It:** Anytime you experience negative emotion, that is your victim-mentality alarm system ringing.
3. **Pick One Thing to Attack:** Identify one solution, even if it's a small improvement, to focus on and attack.

"1 MUST" TAKEAWAY FOR TEAMS

Attacking one solution, even if it's a small solution, will immediately move you from victim mentality to attack mentality.

Part III

Dynasty Level: Rarefied Air

Dynasties weather fierce competition and thrive on adversity. The main ingredients are discussed in Chapters 7, 8, and 9.

Chapter 7

TALENT: SELECTION AND DEVELOPMENT

Talent: The skill level that predisposes a person or a team for success

How important is talent?

Ask any coach in any sport, and he or she will mention some form of the same answer—that without it, you can't consistently win.

But at the same time, the best organizations understand that it isn't the most *absolute* talent that consistently wins. It's the ability to identify an individual's talents, put those talents to the most productive work, and then help those individuals develop and grow those talents.

Yes, Nick Saban perennially has the best recruiting classes in college football at Alabama. He has lots of talent. But he's also doing more with that talent—putting them in position to win—and growing that talent into a fleet of NFL-ready players.

It's safe to say that if you transplanted Saban onto an otherwise mediocre team, he'd figure out how to maximize the talent already there and get to work identifying and growing more talent.

Talent selection and development is every bit as important in business as it is in sports—and there have been thousands of pages printed in management books and manuals filled with exotic methods for picking the right people.

What we've found is that the process doesn't have to be extremely complicated—either for the leader who is looking to get the right people on the bus or the team member who is interested in growing his or her talents.

Jason once asked the great University of Iowa wrestling coach Dan Gable this question: "If you had to choose between having an athlete with talent or one with a great work ethic, what would you choose?" Gable, with a sly grin, responded, "I choose the athlete with both."

We should probably start by defining exactly what "talents" are. Let's say you're scouting a quarterback for your football team. The player you're looking at will have a bunch of different talents. He might have a strong arm, a fast time in the forty-yard dash, and plenty of height to see over the line of scrimmage. He also might be smart, a gym rat, and somebody who is super-coachable. All of those talents are part of that player's package.

As that same athlete works his way through college, he could well pick up some other talents. He could learn how to operate in a pro-style offense, for example. He might be responsible for calling his own plays at the line of scrimmage, and become more adept at making those decisions with the experience he gains over time. He could become a vocal team leader in the locker room as he learns to navigate social situations and build relationships.

In other words, some talents you're born with, while others can be learned, improving with practice. Either way, with effort and preparation, all talent can be developed.

In the business world, innate tools are more about intelligence, personality, and work ethic. Some people are better at crunching numbers than others. Some have a more natural way with people, or an almost superhuman level of determination.

So how do you identify what talents people have, and select the right ones for your organization? And if you're already on the team, how do you develop the talents you have—and grow the ones you might not yet have?

We'll start with an illuminating story from the beginning of Jason's time with the St. Louis Cardinals.

TALENT SELECTION—OPTIMISM AND GROWTH MINDSET

In early 2007, the Cardinals were hard at work preparing for the upcoming draft, and the goal was clear. They wanted to do the very best job out of all the Major League Baseball clubs at identifying the hidden talent throughout the draft. Meeting this goal would fill the team's farm system with great players and eventually help the Major League club win more games.

The problem?

Every other team had the same goal, and each of them, like the Cardinals, had a scouting department out there beating the bushes—evaluating the potential stars and trying to uncover the diamonds in the rough.

Historically, professional scouting in baseball had been a decidedly "old-school" pastime. Veteran baseball men would cover their assigned areas and identify talented players from game films and from the stands of high school baseball diamonds. They'd write up reports grading prospects on their throwing, hitting, fielding, and pitching, and they'd make guesses about how their bodies would fill out and how their attitudes and mental makeup would translate to pro ball.

Teams had been doing it that way for more than one hundred years, and virtually every team did it the same way. So it must be working, right?

Well, yes and no.

Good players were obviously making their way into the system, but a close study of the scouting reports—and how they matched up with the performance of the recruits as professional players—revealed something interesting.

Studies showed that scouts paid an inordinate amount of attention to how tall a player was, or how good-looking he was—if the player "looked like a ballplayer."

Unfortunately, those characteristics had shown no significant correlation to success on the field. Height and good looks tell you no more about whether a person would be a good baseball player than they do about whether someone would be a good computer programmer, plumber, or airline pilot.

Throughout the 2000s, scouting became much more sophisticated—more about a player's measurables, mental makeup, and advanced statistics. It was this "new-school" mentality that led to the Cardinals hiring Jason Selk to consult on player selection and development.

Three months before the 2007 draft, the Cardinals' front-office team—led by senior analyst and former NASA engineer Sig Mejdal—asked Jason if he knew of any mental indicators of success that could be identified by the scouting staff and taken into consideration when evaluating players.

At this point, there was virtually no research available on predictive mental characteristics for professional athletes. Jason decided he would try to help the Cardinals build their own model.

His first instinct was to look into "optimism" as one of the predictive characteristics. Jason had studied the work of Dr. Martin Seligman, the famous University of Pennsylvania researcher who is considered the pioneer of positive psychology. Seligman had long established the fact that optimistic people are significantly happier, healthier, and more successful than their pessimistic peers. As he dug deeper into the research, cross-referencing some of the current approaches being used in corporate executive selection, Jason found confirming information from Daniel Goleman in his influential book *Emotional Intelligence*.

Jason contacted Dr. Seligman about his findings, and Dr. Seligman referred Jason to one of his protégés, Stanford researcher Dr. Carol Dweck. At the time, Dr. Dweck was in the process of finishing her first book—*Mindset*, which has since become a huge international bestseller.

In *Mindset*, Dweck established the two different kinds of mindsets that have now become staples in sorting high- and low-achieving people. A "growth" mindset characterizes a person who responds to a challenge by embracing effort and training instead of relying on his or her innate abilities. A "fixed"-mindset person fears failure and avoids new challenges because of how "failure" reflects on him or her personally.[1]

In an interview, Dweck explained it this way: "In a fixed mindset students believe their basic abilities, their intelligence, their talents, are just fixed traits. They have a certain amount and that's that. . . . In a growth mindset students understand that their talents and abilities can be developed through effort, good teaching and persistence."[2]

After several conversations with Dr. Dweck, the Cardinals built a model that boiled down to a few questions that scouts could ask every potential pick to try to identify the ones with both an optimistic and growth mindset. The Cardinals believed they could create a distinct advantage by better identifying players with a growth mindset. They surmised that "growth"-mindset prospects would try harder than their "fixed"-mindset counterparts. The questions went something like this:

1. You do exceptionally well in competition.

   A. I felt very strong during the competition.

   B. I am good at this sport.

2. You are struggling to make improvements in your training.

   A. The technique I am using won't work in the long-run.

   B. The technique I tried doesn't work.

3. You start the season with three losses.

   A. This sport is difficult.

   B. The first part of my schedule was hard.

4. You win a competition for which you have been preparing for a long time.

   A. I had a good day.

   B. I train hard.

5. You can learn new things, but you can't really change your basic athletic ability.

   > Strongly Agree
   > Agree
   > Mostly Agree
   > Mostly Disagree
   > Disagree
   > Strongly Disagree

6. Athletic ability is _____% natural talent and _____% effort/practice (the two percentages should add up to 100%).

The answers indicating an optimistic growth mindset?

1. A
2. B
3. B
4. B
5. Strongly Disagree
6. Anything lower than 51 percent in the first box.

In 2016, *Sporting News* ranked the Cardinals organization as one of the top in baseball, complimenting its "steady stream of talent through sharp-eyed drafting." The team consistently competes at the highest level with core players who have been developed through the team's own farm system.

FIND YOUR "FIT"

When you watch something like the baseball or NFL draft, it can make talent identification and selection seem like something that's almost instantaneous. Somebody is on the clock, and they have five minutes to make the pick. But in reality, teams take months to identify and interview players, putting them through a variety of tests to help come to a decision.

One of the biggest mistakes organizations make is rushing the hire of a new member of a team—especially if that new team member is replacing somebody who was very productive. A sense of crisis often puts pressure on people to make decisions faster and with less preparation than they should use.

Is there a rule of thumb for how long talent selection should take? No, but we often think of it like (don't laugh) dating.

It's easy to go on a single date and be fooled about who the person across from you really is and what he or she is really like. You don't know after an hour what it would actually be like to be in a relationship.

Four dates will give you a much better idea of the person's strengths and weaknesses, and you begin to get a look into his or her fundamental core. It comes down to the channel capacity we discussed earlier in the book. When you have to concentrate on something once, for a set period of time, you can do it. When you add more variables, you'll eventually "break," and your true character will be revealed.

By increasing the interactions—and changing them around—you're encouraging the person to reveal who they really are.

This will often manifest itself in the interview process. When adding people to your respective teams, we suggest you conduct no fewer than four interviews, and each of them should happen in a different kind of setting. One might be in a basic office space, while another will be out at lunch or dinner, or even in a social setting like a bar or office party. Again, exposing people to different environments overwhelms their channel capacity and allows you to get a truer sense of who they are.

The questions you ask should be designed more to identify the person's talents and traits than to get them elaborating on static stuff from their resume. Former GE CEO Jack Welch used a process he called 4-Es and 1-P.

- **Energy:** Are you a high-energy person?
- **Energize Others:** Do you help bring out positive energy in others?
- **Edge:** Can you make tough decisions without seeking others' approval?
- **Execution:** Do you have a track record of delivering/winning?
- **Passion:** What are you passionate about?

Research confirms that one of the greatest predictors of future success through the interview process is how much effort the candidate put into researching the interviewing organization. Taking the time to study up on the potential employer shows initiative and willingness to work, two very important qualities.

Here are some examples of good interview questions:

1. What do you know about our organization?

2. What are the three greatest strengths that you would potentially bring to this organization? (Please give concrete examples of how you have used those in the past to bring value and how you see that playing out with our team.)

3. What is your one biggest need for improvement? (Please give an example of how that played out in a previous setting and how you see that impacting our team.)

NEEDS AND WANTS

As we discussed at the beginning of this chapter, the absolute talent level a team has collectively is secondary to the way the talent on the team fits together and how it fits the challenges it faces.

You *need* talent, and you need the *right* talent.

The system the Cardinals used was designed to identify players who would thrive in their specific organization. Their goal was to find players who would immediately contribute to real, measurable on-field hitting, pitching, and fielding production. GE was looking for people with the 4-E's and 1-P. The company developed questionnaires, created interview questions, and even watched potential candidates in informal settings as a means of identifying the best fit for talent.

You can use some of those same principles, but your goal really should be to create a method that identifies talent specific to the challenges you face.

What does that look like?

Think about it this way: In any given relationship, it is almost impossible to get everything you are looking for. Humans are human and nobody is perfect. This is why 50 percent of marriages end in divorce. A good way to set the stage for success is to identify the three greatest needs and three greatest wants.

For example, in a marriage, a person might say, "I *need* my partner to be faithful, a good parent, and hard working. I *want* my partner to be attractive, to be funny, and to have the same hobbies I do." The needs you have are important enough that it is truly a deal breaker if you don't have all three of them. Again, it's not fair to expect a person to be absolutely perfect in the needs criteria; however, they should show significant strengths in those areas.

In terms of the wants, you might think more like "two out of three ain't bad," or maybe even put them on a 1–10 scale. The person might average out at about a 7. When it comes to needs, a 9 or better is the goal.

Questions to consider:

1. What are the three greatest needs and three greatest wants in terms of talent selection for our organization?
2. Do we have a proven interviewing process that clearly identifies the desired traits?

SELECTION IS IMPORTANT— DEVELOPMENT IS ESSENTIAL

The financial crisis that began in 2008 is probably still fresh in your mind, but the one in 1987 was just as dire. The Dow Jones Industrial Average dropped 22.9 percent in one day, and the business environment for financial advisors was incredibly challenging.

Business, to say the least, was difficult.

In July 1990, Tom Bartow and his fellow partner Dave Clapp took an unusual approach to developing advisors. Instead of investing time and money into advisors in the early stages of their careers, they would invest that time and money into talented advisors who were more experienced and already somewhat successful in the business.

At the time, Tom was reading *Made in America*, a book about Wal-Mart's Sam Walton. In it, there was a description of the vacations Walton would take every year with his family. He'd hit the road in the car and stop anywhere he saw a discount store. His goal was to learn something from every visit he made, to every store. What were each of those stores doing right, and how could he incorporate it into what he was doing?[3]

Tom took the same approach. At a week-long advanced training program at the University of Pennsylvania's Wharton School of Business, he told his fellow Edward Jones attendees that he was going to go off-script and go to one of the "Veteran Advisor Training Sessions" being run by one of Edward Jones's main competitors. He wanted to know what Merrill Lynch was doing right, and how its best advisors operated—so he could bring that knowledge back and share it with his people.

The big lesson Tom learned from the breakout session at Wharton was this: **"When you invest money in rookies you are investing dollars hoping to get pennies in return. When you invest in proven talent you invest pennies and get dollars in return."** This is a direct quote from the legendary Merrill Lynch manager Phil Blevins.

What happens when you invest in experienced people? It sends a distinct message down through the rest of the organization.

That people—and talent—are valued.

There's certainly an accountability that comes with that—for everybody from leaders to team members. If people on the team know they'll be supported and rewarded for continual growth and improvement, you build incredible culture and performance.

Tom and a core group of other experienced executives (Dave Clapp, Chris Gilkison, and Paul Daniels) launched a program they called "TOP GUN." The emphasis was on executing best practices like the ones we shared in our previous book, *Organize*

Tomorrow Today, and earlier in this one—honoring channel capacity, managing expectations, point and flow, recognizing victories—but doing it with more experienced advisors in the firm. This was the introduction of what is now referred to as "Advanced Training" at Edward Jones.

When it comes to Advanced Training and talent development, Edward Jones is still looked at as the gold standard in the industry. The company has proved that investing in talented people within the organization yields massive returns in production and leadership. Many Edward Jones leaders today are graduates of "TOP GUN."

What does this look like in the world of sports? You'll see it when a team brings in a veteran with championship experience and a reputation for being good in the locker room. The general manager and coach want somebody who can come in and help show the way to the younger, less experienced players. When you see what's possible, it all becomes much more real and attainable.

Every organization is under pressure not only to perform, but also to contain costs. And it's so tempting to address the cost issue by being willing to let your more experienced (and often more expensive) contributors go. There are a lot of elements that go into making personnel decisions, but we've found that a simple rule that applies to investing also works when thinking about the relative cost and value of the people making up your team. You can invest dollars in your players and make pennies in return. Or you can invest pennies and get dollars in return.

PENNIES FOR DOLLARS
OR DOLLARS FOR PENNIES

Whenever you see one of those career retrospectives about a player like Michael Jordan, it's so interesting to compare what a player looked like at the beginning of his career to how he matured through to the end. When you see Jordan as a twenty-one-year-old rookie, fresh out of North Carolina, two things will probably jump out at you. He could literally fly. And he was incredibly skinny.

Jordan was a sensation from the minute he arrived in Chicago, and it would have been easy for the Chicago Bulls organization to have said, "Leave this guy alone, don't screw him up." If that had been the case, Jordan would have still had a nice career.

But the Bulls and Jordan did something different.

Through the years, Jordan packed on muscle, becoming a physical specimen. He improved his defense to the point where he was considered the best defender in the NBA. He improved every other skill in his repertoire, including his passing—which got the rest of his team more involved in the game.

He transitioned from a raw scorer early in his career—the guy who would score fifty points in a playoff game and watch his team still lose—to a player who filled up the box score a dozen different ways and led the team to championships.

Six of them.

Not everybody is Michael Jordan, obviously. But every player in every organization—in sports or business—has a set of skills that got them there. And yet the world isn't static. You need to continue to develop your skills so you can stay relevant—and, more importantly, stay passionate about what you're doing.

If you quit improving, you get stale. And when you get stale, you lose interest.

This message is just as important for extremely talented high achievers as it is for complete beginners.

Michael Jordan? He could have coasted on his talent.

This point was driven home for Tom years ago, when he was headed to a UCLA basketball game with his uncle, the former

UCLA coach Gene Bartow. They went early, because Tom's uncle wanted to meet with legendary Los Angeles Laker great Jerry West. West had a Hall of Fame career as a player, and he would go on to have an equally impressive career as a front-office executive.

Tom assumed somebody of West's stature would want to slip into the game after it started, so that he wouldn't have to deal with crowds of people. But West was there an hour before tip, watching the players go through their routines.

Tom waited until the players left the floor to go to the locker room before the game to ask West if he would be willing to share what he was looking for in the players he was scouting.

"I'm here because I want to see how hard they work at improving their skills," West said. "In the NBA, if you don't constantly work at improving your skills, you won't last long."

A lot of scouts would leave early—again, to avoid the crowds—but West stayed for the entire game. "I want to see how smart they play," he said. "We have all kinds of tests we can give them and they might be able to pass those tests in a classroom, but if you don't play smart on the floor, you're going to get us beat."

It didn't take more than a few minutes around West for one main point to be reinforced. **No matter what skill level you fit into, you need to be working on developing those skills and adding others.**

The brutal truth is most organizations focus much more on talent selection than they do on talent development. When they do focus their efforts on development, it's either with the rookies or with the broken players who are performing under potential. The priority with all organizations should be to develop the best players. Invest pennies into your best players, and your team will reap dollars in return.

KNOWING WHAT TO IMPROVE

If you are going to create a platform for developing talent, it is essential that you are developing the right skills. If talent development does not happen strategically, there is a high risk of overloading channel capacity, and we know the negative impact that can have.

There should be a prioritized foundation to work from for everyone. This is what many high-level coaches and leaders refer to as "the process."

As previously discussed, it is essential for each member of the team to be aware of what their "3 Most Important" and "1 Must" activities are daily. The "3 Most Important" activities for many are static—they are the same each and every day. These "3 Most Important" daily activities are known as "process goals."

For example, a financial advisor's process goals might be to make six proactive contacts daily, see one center of influence face-to-face weekly, and get thirty minutes of cardiovascular exercise in daily. A professional golfer may emphasize ten minutes per day of "deep practice" with each club, sixty minutes of strength and conditioning, and a daily mental workout.

Whether you are a golfer on the PGA tour or a financial advisor or anything else, this is where all talent development should begin. **When organizations and individuals work on improving the most important skills, they see the greatest returns.** Our experience with high-level performers is that one small adjustment or improvement to the core process is enough for a person take his or her game to the next level. And the most effective way improve is through self-evaluation.

The most effective self-evaluation questions we have found are:

1. What three things did I do well in the previous twenty-four hours?

2. On a scale of 1–10, how well did I do in the past twenty-four hours completing my "3 Most Important" and "1 Must" tasks?

3. What is one thing I want to improve in the upcoming twenty-four hours?

When individuals self-evaluate daily, improvement will result. To speed up the process of improvement, you can occasionally combine the daily self-evaluation with feedback from a colleague or supervisor. If you're a team leader, simply have teammates evaluate each other and themselves in tandem. Doing so weekly or monthly gives individuals a new perspective on their own performance and talent development.

Sometimes you will find yourself on a plateau with a certain skill. You are working diligently to improve, and for whatever reason, skill development is not happening fast enough. If you're a team leader, you will encounter this frequently with the members of your team. If you've tried a couple of ways to break through the plateau and nothing has worked, that's when it might be a good idea to research other resources that could be of assistance. The resource depends on the skill you're trying to develop, of course. But it's important to see if research or experts on the issue can help. You might get a new perspective on the problem that takes you to a new level.

THE FIFTEEN-MINUTE LEADER-GROWING STRATEGY

The best organizations are designed to funnel smart, motivated people into positions of increased authority. Leaders understand that a big part of their job is creating the stars of the future up and down the organizational chart.

But many organizations either leave this crucial job to chance—and assume that the best aspiring leaders will figure it out themselves—or they follow some complex, convoluted strategy that does more to frustrate everybody involved than to actually identify and grow leadership talent.

We've found that the greatest leaders and the strongest organizations have a set of surprisingly simple techniques for handling this task. After spending time with many of them in sports and business, we've been able to distill it into a set of simple steps useful to anybody who has people working under their supervision.

Set up a fifteen-minute private meeting with each person working under you on your team and ask them to record the following things about the previous three months:

1. What were your three biggest accomplishments?
2. What was the single most important thing you did to make each of those things happen?

As they're making their list, you do the same thing—record what you think their three biggest wins were, and why.

After you receive their list, compare and contrast the lists together—an exercise that will provide a lot of illumination about how the two of you think and prioritize. The lists probably won't be the same, and that's perfectly okay. This is a learning exercise, and getting insight from the front lines is just as valuable for you as it is for the team member to learn what the boss values.

After you've done that, ask the team member to make the same kind of list, but of the three things they would like to do over—and why. Make your own list as they're writing theirs, just as in the first part of the exercise.

Go through the same process with these lists, but keep in mind that people tend to dwell on negatives instead of positives. You want to be spending 75 or 80 percent of your time on the "done wells," vs. 20 or 25 percent on the "do-overs."

The last part of the exercise is to ask what is the most important thing the team member wants to accomplish in the next three months. Does that match with what you expected? Why or why not? If it isn't in line, that's something you can discuss. Maybe the team member is giving you an early look at a productive new line of business, or maybe you'll be in a position where you can suggest a valuable adjustment to his or her plan.

Everybody is learning, and the younger, less-experienced team members are developing some hugely important skills. They're learning how to ask the right questions, and figuring out how to align their personal goals with those of the organization. And the process of going through this exercise is preparing them for the time when they're on the other side of the table, administering those same questions as one of the team leaders.

The veterans on the team are also being forced to improve. This is not only great role modeling for the newer team members, but reinforces the message that learning at all levels is expected and valued.

TEACH IT

When it comes to developing talent, we have one rule: Always have one thing you are trying to improve. The best way to improve the team is to improve yourself.

INVERT

(By inverting any fundamental you can learn more)

When a team doesn't have the right talent or develop its talent, it is investing dollars and getting pennies in return.

"3 MOST IMPORTANT" FOR THE TEAM TO REMEMBER

1. You *need* talent, and you need the *right* talent.
2. When studying other teams or organizations, always identify what they are doing well.
3. Spending pennies developing your best players will return dollars, whereas spending dollars on your lower performers will return pennies.

"1 MUST" TAKEAWAY FOR TEAMS

Investing time and resources in talent development sends a clear message that you care about your people and believe in them and fosters a culture of accountability and continual improvement.

Chapter 8

THE ATTACK MENTALITY: "ATTACK, ALWAYS ATTACK"

Attack Mentality: An extreme focus to the point of obsession

When the Vikings set out to conquer new lands, they would land their ships on the shore, and just before beginning the invasion, they would burn their own ships. Retreat was not an option, only attack.

The business world is full of code words for it.

Energy.

Passion.

Relentlessness.

Drive.

Desire.

Motivation.

All of those words describe the same attitude. Our term for it is the "attack mentality"—which we derived from the quotation by General George S. Patton that became the title of this chapter—and we believe it's one of the main separators between peak performers and average producers.

But General Patton wasn't the only major figure of history who had it. Steve Jobs had it. Mother Teresa was consumed by it.

They all had very different goals, but they had one thing in common: the attack mentality.

For Patton it was about saving American soldiers' lives and inflicting casualties on the enemy. For Steve Jobs it was the unstoppable pursuit of technological advance and excellence in design. For Mother Theresa it was loving the downtrodden. And for Coach Wooden it was the complete mastery of the journey to success, rooted in preparation. Each, in his or her own way, had the attack mentality.

It's not necessary to be a Viking, a general, a genius, a saint, or even the coach of an athletic team to have the attack mentality, but without it you cannot consistently compete at the highest level and reach dynasty status.

Whatever natural advantages the best of the best have, they bring with them one other critical trait, almost without exception: it is this internal fire, this desire for "winning"—however that is defined for them.

What makes this such an important and interesting subject for leaders and teams is that the attack mentality is 100 percent learnable. You can't become a six-foot-five, 285-pound athlete, like J. J. Watt of the Houston Texans, or transplant Steve Jobs's brain into your head.

But if you commit yourself to the right strategies and principles and give an honest effort, you can have for yourself the mentality that produces the true champions. **The attack mentality is a choice as much as it is a trait.** In this chapter, we're going to show you how to "choose it."

IGNITING PASSION

We think "passion" is simple to define, but hard to ignite. Passion is having something you care about. It might be basketball. Or helping people. Or computer coding. The "what" isn't what matters, as long as it's important to you. It sounds like a simple concept, but in our travels to organizations around the country, we see thousands of people who have been beaten down so much by the grind of working that they don't care anymore. The job has become just that—a job—and they're going through the motions. They're doing the work for the money it provides, and they readily admit that they just want to do the work and go home at the end of the day. Within this mindset, it is extremely easy to let go of the wheel and stop caring.

But to reach the dynasty level, your team must care. About something. If "caring" sounds like a foreign language to you, it's time to reignite that passion inside you. To do so, you need to follow a somewhat simple three-step process:

1. Find one thing to care about.
2. Identify your talent.
3. Develop a work ethic.

The first step, identifying something you care about, isn't about finding some new hobby. We don't want to insult you. We assume you are reading this book to help yourself professionally. Certainly, we hope and believe there will be positive carryover into your personal life. But this exercise is all about making you and your team more successful. Answering these three questions will help you identify your passion:

1. In my current job, what three things do I most enjoy?
2. In my current job, what three things am I good at?
3. In my current job, what is one thing I enjoy and am good at?

Did you actually answer the above three questions? The reason we ask is that these days, the act of "thinking" happens less and less often. There are a number of reasons for this trend that we won't go into, but the point is that most people these days are out of the habit of thinking. Because of this, when people are faced with difficult questions, they allow themselves to answer with "I don't know" or "I will figure that out later." You must at times force yourself to care.

Unfortunately, "later" rarely comes. We want to challenge you right now to stop allowing yourself to not think. No more giving yourself permission to not answer tough questions. Don't worry about getting the perfect answer. Perfection is not possible; nor is it necessary. Remember, any answer is better than no answer. By answering, you force yourself to think. **Once the thinking process begins, it typically continues.**

You may not have the right answer, but forcing yourself to answer will much more quickly get you there. If you need to reignite passion, please, for your sake, go back and force yourself to think through the three questions listed on page 163. It's your answer to question number three that will most likely be your place to "attack."

The second step in the process of finding something to care about is to get your mind and body right for reigniting passion. This isn't a place for a health lecture, but if you can commit ninety days to two physical rules, we believe you'll find yourself positioned to have a significant increase in energy and purpose. You'll be ready to care again.

- Avoid alcohol and drug use. (If you do need to drink, limit your drinking to two drinks or less daily.)
- At least four times a week, complete 30 minutes of cardiovascular exercise. In these sessions, your heart rate should average 130 beats per minute. (This advice assumes you are in good health. If you have not been exercising, begin slowly

and work your way up to this goal within forty-five days. Please consult your doctor before you begin to make sure there are no health concerns.)

This prescription isn't particularly complicated, but it does take some commitment and willpower. Think of it as the first step on your way to the new you.

When you've gotten through those ninety days, it might seem like there's no outlet for you to care about something. Maybe you have a less-than-exciting job that isn't your long-term career answer.

But it doesn't matter if you're playing center for the Los Angeles Lakers or stocking shelves at Wal-Mart. There is some aspect of your job where you can declare that you care.

When it comes to finding one thing to care about, you must now increase the expectations you have of yourself and your performance—not in everything you do, but rather in just one specific aspect of your job. If you're the basketball center, you can decide that boxing out your man when a shot goes up is going to be your religion. Nobody is going to care more about getting defensive rebounds than you. It will become your focus, and your workman's pride.

At Wal-Mart, you might challenge yourself to be the most efficient and precise shelf-stocker in your store, and come up with your own metric for measuring that goal. Your caring goal will become your motivation—even if the task is "beneath" you for the time being. The key is to get serious about one thing and to have the expectation that you totally attack your one thing.

Take another moment and answer one more question:

1. What is the one area within my current position where I can set a goal to become the absolute best?

All people with the "attack mentality" have higher expectations of themselves than everyone else. They always have the goal to be consistently improving at something—not at everything, but always at least at one thing. Developing this higher expectation at your one thing will force your attack mentality to develop over time. The focus here should not be on whether you actually are the best, but on being relentless about improving toward reaching that goal. When you force yourself to experience the obsession for improvement, it shows you care, and it ignites your passion.

TALENT: THE PREDISPOSITION OF SUCCESS

The second piece of the puzzle—talent—is another one that gets caught up in plenty of misunderstanding and misinformation. Depending on who you listen to, talent is something that you either have or don't, or it's something that can be developed. Wherever you stand in that argument, you could be discouraged, either because you seemingly won't be able to change anything about your "talent," or because the work it takes to improve your talent is seemingly too hard to accomplish.

Again, we want to take a more direct approach to the subject. In our view, "talent" is nothing more than a niche where you show some predisposition for success. It doesn't mean that you have to show the potential to be Stephen King if you want to be a writer, or Steph Curry if you want to be a point guard. It just means that you show more of a predisposition toward one of those niches than another. It's a starting point.

It stands to reason that if you pick something that you have more of a predisposition for, it will take less work for you to develop the skills that surround that predisposition.

Having talent makes it feel like swimming with the current of the attack mentality. This is not to say that you can't excel at attacking unless you have talent. Not at all. It is just easier if you choose a discipline where talent exists.

The great thing about talent is that it can be developed through effort and perseverance. It's important to remember that no matter what your current level of talent is, it can be increased. **The more you work at something, the more talented you become.**

WORK ETHIC: GRINDING IT OUT . . . WHEN NECESSARY

The third consideration in terms of reigniting passion is work ethic. By now we have all heard the saying "You never have to work if you love what you do." Unfortunately, that is just not true for elite performers. **If you or your team are going to execute at the dynasty level, there will still be days that you will just need to "fight thru" and grind it out.**

Being great isn't supposed to be easy. If being great were easy, everyone would be great, and hence there would be no separation. Being great requires you and your team to do things that others can't or won't do. **Without the "fight-thru" (those days and times when you just don't feel like doing the work), there is no opportunity for greatness.**

It's the days when you need to grind it out that you will begin to see the real difference in performance. It's winning those fight-thru days that will cement in your mind your attack mentality.

This is where the elite performers create most of their distance between themselves and "the rest." If you want to be Tom Brady or Nick Saban or Elon Musk, you have to be willing to do "whatever it takes" to continue to progress toward being the best at your one thing. Some days it might be easy to accomplish your "best at one thing" goal, and other days it will be a monster. No matter, you must have the "whatever it takes" approach if you want to internalize your attack mentality. For you to be the best version of yourself and for your team to reach its potential, that kind of goal needs to be the centerpiece of your mindset.

To this point you have heard us mention many times the concept of your "1 Must." Choosing your one thing to be best at should probably be the same thing as your "1 Must" each day. The rationale behind this is that if you are not passionate about doing your "1 Must" each day, then either it won't get done consistently, or the execution will be poor.

Developing the attack mentality is such an important thing that if your chosen one thing isn't your "1 Must," it's probably a good idea to make them one and the same. Learning to develop an attack mentality will ultimately make you better at *everything*.

There are four techniques you can use to help yourself win those fight-thrus when you don't feel like attacking your one thing.

- **Ritualize:** Do your one thing at the same time every day. This takes the thinking out of the doing. No energy is wasted trying to figure out when it is going to happen each day. When it's time to attack your one thing—get it done—NO EXCUSE.
- **Recognize:** When it's time to attack your one thing and you realize you don't want to do it, simply say to yourself, "I know what's going on here, I am in a fight-thru." Doing so will help you gear up to win the fight.
- **Ask Two Questions:** When you recognize you're in a fight-thru, ask yourself, "How am I going to feel if I win this fight-thru?" and "How am I going to feel if I lose this fight-thru?" Bring as much emotion as possible into your answers. In this case, emotion promotes action.

- **Life Projection:** If, after asking yourself the previous two questions, you still have not mustered the energy to attack, create a clear vision of who you will be and how your life will be in five years if you consistently lose this fight-thru, and then compare that with who you will be and how your life will be in five years if you consistently win this fight-thru. Again, bring as much emotion into the visualization as possible.

When it comes to working hard, **you will find that making yourself uncomfortable speeds up the process of developing mental toughness**. Think about improving your work ethic incrementally. Begin with the goal of being the hardest worker on the team for the first five minutes of the week. Once you have that down, make it your next goal to be the hardest worker in the first five minutes each and every day. Then move to outworking everyone for the first hour of the day. Keep making progress until you are dominating one entire day.

Make progressive improvements over time with work ethic, and your talent and passion will reach new heights.

OBSESSION FOR IMPROVEMENT

At the apex of business and sports, the players and coaches have ultimate responsibility. The scoreboard and stat sheets don't lie. When players and coaches aren't getting it done anymore, they get fired, traded, or released. It's a ruthless process—but one that shows us some important lessons.

Tom Brady's 2016 season is a great example. He was suspended for the first four games of the season because the NFL believed he had conspired with equipment managers for the Patriots to adjust the air level in footballs so they'd be easier to throw. He vigorously protested the charge, fighting the league all the way into court.

Brady could have taken the case even higher in the court system, but he decided to accept the four-game suspension so that he and his team could move on and plan for the season.

Injuries, illness, professional setbacks, and personal problems all create perfect opportunities to make excuses. As we have already discussed, making excuses repeatedly is what establishes a very common mindset—the victim mentality.

When facing adversity, someone who has the victim mentality focuses on the difficulty and unfairness of the adversity instead of the potential pivots and solutions to beat the adversity. People in that position are likely to wallow in the adversity, talking about it endlessly—and potentially spreading it to others.

And unfortunately, the victim mentality is *completely normal.* It is how most people react to a challenge. And it is why most people are just about average. That isn't a criticism. It's an observation of reality.

When Tom Brady and his team faced the adversity of the negative NFL ruling, they could have continued to complain about the unfairness of it—using their huge media platform to do it. They could have sulked, whined, and made excuses.

They did none of that. Instead, they attacked. They kept quiet and worked harder than ever, resolving to be more ready physically and mentally than ever before. They changed their mindset to embrace the four-week suspension as a way to keep their number one quarterback healthy and give a couple backups some much-needed experience and playing time.

You know how the story ends. Brady had one of his greatest seasons, and the team engineered the greatest comeback in Super Bowl history. The New England Patriots—and many other teams and organizations—demonstrate that the victim mentality is only a recipe for mediocrity and "averageness."

Truth is, every team that has ever achieved any significant level of success has had to reject the victim mentality vehe-

mently. Individuals or team members who view themselves as victims will become victims. **Even when life has thrown unfair circumstances at you, you must never allow yourself to feel like your situation is unfair or unjust.** Everyone experiences adversity and traumatic events. Everyone. It is a part of life for all of us.

Some people certainly have it harder than others, and we would never deny that, but that's not the focus here. It's all about having the right mindset and giving yourself a chance to win no matter how the cards are stacked against you.

It is not possible to have the attack mentality and the victim mentality at the same time. **In the face of adversity, you and your team will either choose to be "victims" or choose to "attack."** Learn to choose wisely.

Compare the words of two of Jason's clients, one of the best players in the history of the NHL and the CEO of one of the biggest commercial real estate companies in the world.

The hockey player:

There's no doubt that the main reason I've been so successful is because I am obsessed with being the best. Even when I was young and totally undersized, I knew I didn't want to be average. I couldn't be average. It just wasn't acceptable. So I started searching for ways to get an edge. It started with stick-handling and shooting accuracy, and eventually moved to being more physically and mentally prepared than my opponents. That's still the case today. I refuse to let somebody out-work me.

And the real estate developer:

I started with nothing and worked my way up the ladder. There was a point in my career when I was leveraged far more than I was comfortable, and I had to make a decision. I was face-to-face with the reality that I could lose everything, or I could get really serious and commit to making it work. For a couple of years, it was really, really bad. I was getting up at 4 in the morning and going to bed late at night. Even though it was scary, I knew I could make it through if I could just keep it up. And sure enough, I stayed with it and it paid off. It wasn't really much of a decision, honestly, because going back to nothing was not a reality I could live with.

Those two are examples from super-high achievers, but it happens on a day-to-day basis in all kinds of organizations. As a leader with the attack mentality, you must believe in your people. You must have extremely high expectations of their fortitude and ability.

This attitude must be displayed through a positive "I believe in you" lens. It cannot be communicated in a demeaning or angry manner. For example, **"I know you can do this" will be much more well received than "What is wrong with you?" or "Why are you underperforming like this?"**

Individuals must have this same kind of self-belief in themselves. It means holding yourself to a higher standard and talking to yourself through the positive filter of "I know I can do this," as opposed to "I'm not good enough."

APPLYING THE ATTACK MENTALITY

Everyone experiences the victim mentality. It's important to know how to immediately move from victim to attack. It's all about recognizing and identifying. You must first recognize that you are face-to-face with the victim mentality. Something bad has happened, and it seems unfair, almost as though the odds against you are insurmountable. In those situations, learn to say to yourself, "I know what is going on here. The victim mentality is trying to get me."

Once you recognize that the victim-mentality invitation is in your hand, decide to tear up that invitation. Reject it, fight it, and get back to attack mode by picking just one thing to get all over.

Jason was working with an NFL team, and they were getting prepared for a game where the temperatures would be pushing 100 degrees at game time. The savvy head coach of the team overheard one of his coaches commenting on the upcoming week's game and the fact that it was going to be "tough playing in that kind of heat."

Even though it was a road game, the head coach immediately recognized the victim mentality setting in. Instead of going with it, he decided to use the heat as an opportunity to get an edge. The goal was to take advantage of the heat by being more conditioned for it—both physically and mentally. The players were going to thrive on the heat, while the opponent dealt with cramps and exhaustion.

It started on Monday. Every player was instructed to double his fluid intake, and specific nutrition plans were handed out. Trainers and medical staff were asked to be present for all practices and to be on the lookout for any health concerns. The players were to wear multiple layers of clothes under their pads during practices, and the thermostat at the indoor practice facility was turned up.

The one key activity for the week was to control the players' self-talk about the heat. Jason instructed them to say to themselves, "I am an absolute beast. The hotter it gets, the stronger I become."

Throughout the tough week of practice, the players repeated that mantra every time they started to feel sorry for themselves about how hot it was. It set the stage for one of the best weeks of practice of the season, and the team easily won its game in the heat.

Anytime you find yourself feeling like a victim, all you need to do to get into the attack mentality is to pick that one thing—the one thing that will best allow you to work through and actually take advantage of the adversity. Pick that one thing, and totally commit to nailing it until it moves you through the adversity.

Sometimes, you have to know when to be flexible, of course. If, instead of heat, the team's practice area was surrounded by fires, you wouldn't ask your team to play with an unhealthy level of smoke. Nor would you ask an injured player to "fight thru" the pain, causing the injury to get worse. With that kind of adversity, you have to have common sense and find other solutions. The key to remember is that to move from victim mindset to attack mentality, all you need is to find one thing within your control to totally attack.

We're not implying that this is simple. Frankly, it's not. Moving from the victim mindset to be on the attack is difficult. What we are saying is that it can be done, and it's critical for you and your team to work on this mindset skill. It's like anything else: the more you work on it, the better you will become.

FROM THE TOP

If you're responsible for a team, you have two main jobs when it comes to promoting an attack attitude. You have to do a good job selecting team members who have passions that align with the team, and you must help individuals identify the one thing they can attack daily.

Identifying passion is just the first step of the process. You also have to be able to articulate those passions simply and repeatedly to the team. As we've been discussing in the previous chapters, messages get garbled and they get forgotten. This isn't the time to get fuzzy, careless, or casual.

If you could talk to any football player who has played under Nick Saban at Alabama or Bill Belichick in New England, you'd hear them reference the saying "Do Your Job" multiple times. It was the code phrase—and main responsibility—of each member of the team. The coaching staff devises the plans, giving each player specific jobs to do. Then they train them in how to do their jobs.

Each member knows the one most important thing they can do to help the team achieve its ultimate goals. That information is clearly directed and repeated over and over throughout training: minicamps, preseason, regular season, and playoffs.

How were players recognized and rewarded? For how well and how consistently they did their jobs, how well they nailed their one most important thing daily. As a player, if your passion was attacking your one most important activity each day, you were going to have a very successful career with Coach Saban or Coach Belichick.

It isn't a surprise, then, that Saban and Belichick (or Coach John Wooden before them) do not automatically take the players everybody would consider the consensus "best." Sure, Alabama and UCLA had plenty of blue-chip prospects, and Belichick's Patriots don't have a bunch of free agent rejects running around out there.

But those coaches—and all great team leaders—understand that selecting the *right* team members doesn't always mean selecting the ones with the highest raw measurables. That salesman who did $5 million in business last year? Maybe he doesn't play well with others in a team setting. Adding him to a sales group tasked with doing a big team presentation for a giant client might be a recipe for disaster.

As the leader, you need to ask yourself about every potential addition to the team: How much alignment does this person have with what you're trying to accomplish? You don't need perfect alignment among the members with the team's top one or two passions, but there needs to be alignment with at least one of them. The more alignment there is, the easier it will be to instill the attack mentality.

If you find a potential team member who is in complete alignment with the team's passions, you've found somebody who has the potential to be a team leader himself or herself someday—like Tom Brady became for the Patriots.

SEDUCTION OF SUCCESS

If you and your team improve even slightly on the attack mentality, there will be a significant increase in success. Unfortunately, most people respond to success by taking their foot off the gas. It's the old phenomena of "it worked so well I stopped doing it."

The great teams have learned to use success rather than be seduced by it. **The best time to make the move to the next level is when you have the momentum of success working in your favor.** Think about it: when things are going well, when you are attacking the work and seeing results, that is when you actually have the energy to push down on the gas just a bit more.

When a team is already winning and applies the attack mentality to an even higher degree, major separation occurs—the gap between that team and the rest widens dramatically. The technique to remember is "a little bit more for a little while." When you sense yourself or the team being seduced by success, that is the time to pick one key activity and do up to 10 percent more that day.

Jason saw the impact of "a little bit more for a little while" play out with one of his clients in the PGA. This young man was quickly becoming a rising star on the tour, and it had everything to do with his attack mentality. He had a meticulously planned out preparation routine that included a healthy combination of skill-specific focus with strength and conditioning. His daily mantra was "I outwork the competition every day. I am always more physically and mentally prepared."

And to his credit, it appeared that was the case. He was relentless about getting the work in every day. The work was paying off, he was making more and more cuts, and he was consistently having "significant money finishes."

He followed the rule that no matter what, he would complete his workouts and preparation plan in full. In addition, every tournament where he made the cut, the very next week his preparation would include an extra ten minutes per day of something called "deep practice." In his extra time of "deep practice," he would simulate as best he could the pressure conditions that he just successfully played through in the previous last day of the tournament.

Jason asked him about the impact of doing extra deep practice after success and he responded by saying, "It's actually a little easier for me to do a little more when I'm winning. I'm not as tight, it's not as much of a grind. It definitely boosts my confidence."

When normal people start winning, they have tendency to do a little bit less attacking. **When mentally tough people experience success, they figure out the number one most important reason for the success, and then they attack just a little bit more on that one thing.** That is the single biggest difference between people who win occasionally and those who win consistently.

GETTING STARTED

If you're new to a team, learning how to have the attack mentality can seem like an overwhelming task—especially if you've never done it before. But as we discussed in the beginning of this chapter, it's something you can learn. It happens just like learning most things—one inch at a time.

Some of this will feel uncomfortable, but that's okay. It's a learning process, and it will feel more comfortable as time goes on. Make sure your expectations are in order.

If you were learning to ride a motorcycle, you wouldn't jump on and go immediately to the expressway for a 70-mph ride. You'd start with the basics, in a controlled environment.

That is what you do here, too.

Begin with something totally controllable and productive. If you are going to put your energy into something, you might as well make it worthwhile for yourself. Ask yourself this question: What is the one activity that would have the most impact on me reaching my goals and the team's goals? Whatever that one thing is, commit to attacking it for five minutes daily. Do this for a few days, and when you are comfortable with the five-minute attack session, go up to six or seven minutes. Have a goal to eventually get to sixty minutes of attack mentality.

Anyone who attacks his or her one most important activity for sixty minutes daily is bound for success. Sound too good to be true? Try it. We have seen it too many times now to question it. It will work, and you and your team will love the results.

TEACH IT

Find one thing to attack each and every day, even if for just five minutes, to push toward excellence. Attacking consistently breeds the attack mentality. The more ingrained the attack mentality becomes, the more you and your team will thrive on it.

When in doubt, follow General Patton's rule: "Attack, Always Attack."

INVERT

(By inverting any fundamental you can learn more)

A team without an attack mentality never reaches its potential.

"3 MOST IMPORTANT" FOR THE TEAM TO REMEMBER

1. It is not necessary to be a general, a genius, a saint, or a coach to have the attack mentality, but without it you will never compete at the highest level. Whatever job you have, no matter your role, you can always leave a mark of excellence, and to do so you will need an attack mentality.
2. To truly have an attack mentality, you must have an obsession for improvement on at least one thing. You must strive for being the best at that one thing: do not accept anything less than relentlessly striving to improve toward reaching your potential at your one thing.
3. At times, grinding it out will be a necessity. That's when you must remember every time you win a "fight-thru," you make it easier to win the next "fight-thru."

"1 MUST" TAKEAWAY FOR TEAMS

Anytime you catch yourself or your team falling prey to the victim mentality, you can immediately move to the attack mindset by picking one thing and attacking (even if for just five minutes).

Chapter 9

ADJUSTMENTS: WHAT, WHEN, AND HOW

Team Adjustments: Collective changes in direction, strategy, or mindset to promote improved team performance

Abraham Maslow may have said it best: "To a man who only has a hammer, everything he encounters looks like a nail."

What does this actually mean?

It means that people who have only one tool don't usually adapt to a situation. They make the situation adapt to them. As you can imagine, this method of approaching challenges isn't likely to be very successful.

At times, some of the great teams we've worked with looked very different from each other from the outside. But regardless of what those teams looked like and how they were made up, they had a common thread relating to adaptability: one of the big differences between very successful teams and dynasties lies in the ability to make adjustments.

Great teams are solid to the core when it comes to the fundamentals of their business or sport, but dynasties are fundamentally sound *and* tremendously flexible. They don't rely on just one signature method or move to win.

You might have a terrific method of making a sale, scoring points, or building a relationship. But if your solution is always the same, you're the person with a hammer.

Can a hammer work? Sure. There are nails out there. But the person who has a full toolbox can not only drive the nail, but also solve more complex problems that require other strategies. And he or she can also solve those problems more efficiently.

Ask yourself a question. Could you build a house from scratch with just a hammer? Could you compete on the professional golf tour with just a driver? Could you win the Cy Young Award for the league's best pitcher by throwing fastballs over and over again?

ONLY THE PARANOID SURVIVE

If you're looking for the equivalent of an elite professional sports team in the business world, the Intel of the 1970s and early 1980s would be a great example. Formed in 1968 by chemist Gordon Moore and physicist Robert Noyce, one of the coinventors of the microchip, the company quickly grew to include chemical engineer Andy Grove—who would eventually end up becoming the company's CEO.

Intel would dominate the early era of computer memory, building market-leading chips for the vast majority of personal and business computers. But by the early 1980s, the market was changing. Cheaper memory from Japanese companies was flooding the market, and Intel's very existence was challenged.

In his book *Only the Paranoid Survive*, Grove wrote that he and Moore had an epiphany in 1985—after a year floundering to find a new corporate strategy. "We were discussing our quandary, and our mood was downbeat," Grove said. "I turned to Gordon and asked, 'If we get kicked out and the board brings in a new CEO, what do you think he would do?'"

Grove went on: "Gordon answered without hesitation. 'He would get us out of memories.'"[1]

Instead of waiting for the axe to fall, Grove and Moore pivoted Intel—the world leader in memory chips—to focus on the microprocessor business. That led to almost two decades of unprecedented profits as one of the main suppliers to IBM for its personal computers. Intel microprocessors were so ubiquitous that computers that ran them had logos on the front that proclaimed "Intel Inside."

Grove and company had created a true dynasty by being willing to make adjustments.

Roy Williams is an example of those who qualify as college basketball coaching royalty. He was a volunteer student assistant under Dean Smith at North Carolina, and came back as a regular paid assistant to Smith from 1978 to 1988. In 1989, Williams took the job at Kansas—one of college basketball's premier programs—and took the team to two national championship games.

In 2003, Williams took over at North Carolina, his alma mater. Since then, his teams have won three national championships—in 2005, 2009, and 2017. His perspective on the game is fascinating and comprehensive, because he came up under the very "old-school" Dean Smith and now thrives in the modern game.

"Your game plan is only good for the first six minutes of the game," Williams says about the ability to adapt in-game. "The rest is about adjustments. As a coach, you have to be able to make strategic adjustments—but just as important, you must help your team make the mental adjustments that need to be made to manage the momentum of competition."

That's exactly what North Carolina did in the 2017 title game against Gonzaga—both in the big picture and within the context of the game itself. Many of North Carolina's players had been a part of the previous season's brutal last-second loss to Villanova in the championship game. They resolved to get back and complete the journey successfully the next season.

In Gonzaga, they were facing the number one team in the country, which came into the game with a record of 37–1. The number two Tarheels gave up 13 early points to Josh Perkins, but after making some halftime adjustments, held Perkins scoreless in the second half. North Carolina's emotional leader, point guard Joel Berry, played the game on two sprained ankles, but he still scored 22 points and assisted on the dunk that put the game away in the final seconds.

Both Grove and Williams were able to master the "how" and "when" to make effective adjustments, and they were able to communicate those adjustments effectively to their teams. The team members had the mindset and training to be in position to receive the game plan and the adjustments and make them on the fly.

They achieved consistency through adjustments.

TWO TYPES OF ADJUSTMENTS

There are "strategic" adjustments and there are "mental" adjustments. **Strategic adjustments are changes in the approach, process, or method of conducting business. Mental adjustments are changes in attitude or perspective.**

In business and sports, both kinds of adjustments are necessary. The key is figuring out which adjustments are needed and mastering when and how to make those adjustments effectively.

As famous football coach and leadership guru Bill Walsh said, "In the NFL everybody has a game plan. The difference at our level is how you execute your backup plan." In sports, teams go into every game with a game plan, but they also anticipate the need to make adjustments, and they have adjustment plans ready to insert when necessary. The same can be done in business. Here are a few examples:

- **All-Day Meetings:** If you are in charge, you must always be ready to make an adjustment based on the energy level of the audience.
- **The Big Presentation:** Arrive early enough to scope out the audience, room size, and technology capabilities. Be prepared to make changes to your presentation content or delivery based on these factors.
- **Prospecting Contact:** When it becomes evident that the prospect is hoping you can deliver value in a different manner than originally anticipated, you must adjust your pitch to focus on their needs and wants.

The key point we are trying to make is this: **always have a back-up plan**. When we work with different organizations to help improve their performance, one interesting fact almost always stands out. In virtually every organization's efforts, the primary focus is on making *strategic* adjustments to achieve improved results.

Some of these organizations have moved people from job to job, or added or subtracted staff. They have changed people's job responsibilities, or reorganized the way products were built, marketed, or sold. They have changed *stuff*—this is the most common type of adjustment, a strategic adjustment.

Strategic adjustments are behavioral in nature. The Intel story about changing from memory to microprocessor is a great example of a strategic adjustment. Changing the activities around in an all-day meeting, including a more relevant story in a big presentation, or reformulating a sales pitch: these are all examples of strategic adjustments.

The second type of adjustment is a mental adjustment, a change in how a person or team thinks. **In business, strategic adjustments are common, while mental adjustments are seldom the emphasis.** Here's a fact of life: most organizations don't make mental adjustments. And this is why very few of them reach the dynasty level.

Mental adjustments are simple in nature but seldom tried in business. A mental adjustment is made when an individual changes his or her perspective concerning the benefit, the purpose, or the rationale of the needed strategic adjustment. **A mental adjustment is the "why" behind the change in approach.**

Mental adjustments are more important than strategic adjustments because they serve as the fuel and conviction for the execution of the strategic adjustment as well as the follow-through. Most organizations just leave the mental adjustment part out and move right to ordering people around and making them do different things in their jobs.

Strategic adjustments generally require huge amounts of time, energy, and resources. It took Intel about two years—and millions of dollars—to execute its strategy change. Mental adjustments take much less time, energy, and resources and lead to faster and more efficient results. In Intel's case, the mental adjustment occurred when Andy Grove asked Gordon Moore what a new CEO would do. They both realized the benefit of moving from memories into microprocessors—and the consequences if they didn't.

Understanding this reasoning was essential for the company's eventual success and for the efficiency of the transition at every turn. Grove and Moore knew why they were making such a big adjustment, and they communicated its importance effectively to the members of the team. Because they communicated their reasoning, the entire team was on board, with increased conviction about the company's vision and goals. The adjustment turned a successful memory company into one of the greatest tech giants in the history of business.

When you make a strategic adjustment, you can speed up the process by making a corresponding mental adjustment. **Dynasty-like organizations combine strategic adjustments with mental adjustments.**

YOU CANNOT FORCE A CHANGE IN ATTITUDE

Colonel Ed Hubbard of the US Air Force, who was a prisoner of war in North Vietnam for 2,420 days from 1966 to 1973, is one of the true heroes in American history. As mentioned earlier, he wrote about his experiences in his book *Escape from the Box*.

Hubbard described what the regular torture routine was from his North Vietnamese guards—beatings with clubs, rubber hoses, and water-soaked ropes. What he said about it would be particularly meaningful for anyone forced to undergo such a harrowing experience: "They could change our behavior whenever they wanted," Hubbard said. "They couldn't change our attitude."[2]

In our everyday lives, we do not face anything like what Hubbard faced. And yet those words are still instructive, not only for individuals, but also for anyone involved in leading a team of any kind: Anybody can give orders and force team members to follow directions. Command and control is relatively easy. But the best teams have team members who share a common *attitude* about the tasks at hand. They understand the team's vision and its short- and long-term goals, and they are in alignment with those goals. They trust what leadership is telling them.

That attitude comes from trusting that the overall direction is the correct one—even if there's some disagreement about the specific tactics to be used to get to the destination.

Attitude changes come when team members see the advantages that will come to them if they follow the new strategic initiatives. When coaches give players guidance, and the guidance makes a play run more efficiently and successfully, it's easy to get everybody's buy-in. Of course, most organizational decisions aren't always so clear-cut.

In the corporate arena, when a strategic adjustment is made without the necessary mental adjustment, one of the more common results is whining and complaining. Instead of whining and complaining, you want your team members to put everything they can into the new plan. How do you get them to that point?

Whining and complaining are the most likely result when people are asked to change behaviors without understanding the reason for the change or the expected benefits. It's important to understand what whining and complaining do to an individual, and in turn to the organization. No matter what the nature of the team, energy is the lifeblood of performance. There is a cost to whining and complaining, and the cost is increased stress and decreased energy. **When a person whines and complains, he or she is self-inflicting stress.** Stress decreases energy.

When someone whines or complains, here's what happens: IT ERODES ENERGY.

With every whine and every complaint, the individual loses precious energy. He or she also loses time. Strange as this may seem, energy is more important than time. Losing them both is an equation for failure.

Unfortunately, whining and complaining are contagious. The more they continue, the more individuals on the team become infected. The losses become exponential.

For a mental adjustment to occur, individuals must be educated on *why* the strategic adjustment needs to be executed. And it must be put in terms of why and how this change will benefit the *individual* team member. Think about Colonel Hubbard and how he made the mental adjustment to survive with dignity, loyalty, and integrity. Once he made that decision, he managed to survive for almost seven grueling years.

Once a person makes the mental adjustment, the likelihood of successful execution of strategic adjustments is significantly increased.

Three questions to consider:

1. In the previous twelve months, what is one strategic adjustment that I (or my team) have made?
2. On a scale of 1–10, how much effort was put into making the mental adjustment in combination with the strategic adjustment?
3. In the upcoming six months, what is one strategic adjustment that I (or the team) should make?

KNOWING "WHAT" TO ADJUST

An extremely effective method for identifying necessary adjustments is to "evaluate with new eyes." You look at something as if you were seeing it for the first time. This is exactly what Andy Grove did when he asked the question "If we get kicked out and the board brings in a new CEO, what do you think he would do?"

Evaluating with new eyes forces you to remove yourself from emotion and established neural patterns. It is an extremely effective method of opening the mind for potential possibilities. Another way to promote mental adjustments is to evaluate your organization through the eyes of your competition. This notion was popularized in Sun Tzu's famous book *The Art of War*. Sun Tzu stated the importance of a specific type of self-evaluation where one is forced to think like the opposition.

Here are two questions to consider:

1. What is the one thing I most hope the competition doesn't do?
2. If I were the opposition, what is the number one thing I would do to attack our organization?

Below are some areas to think about when evaluating whether adjustments are needed, and if so, what kinds of adjustments they might be.

1. **Current Events:** Markets are always changing, and new technology appears every day. Organizations always need to be aware of these trends—but more importantly, leaders and team members need to be constantly asking themselves what trends could be making major impacts on the team's situation one year, three years, and five years down the road.
2. **Personnel Changes:** When current team members are removed, it must be clear who will pick up the slack and how they will do it. When new people are brought in, it is essential to quickly identify their three most important tasks. Whether the team is downsizing or growing, the adjustment must be addressed systematically through the lens of how this change will impact the entire team.
3. **The Calendar:** Some organizations let the calendar dictate the intensity and amount of work being done. Does this sound familiar? At many organizations "the holidays" last for weeks, or the weekend doesn't start after work Friday night—it begins at about 10:00 that morning. People start coasting. In our coaching, we encourage teams to train the

"Friday Mantra" into their mindset—*GET IN, GET AF-TER IT, GET OUT.* This is part of the attack mentality we've been describing since the beginning of the book.

Self-evaluation through new eyes and through the eyes of the opposition causes you to identify new ideas about how to attack the competition and how to best defend against possible threats. Unfortunately, most people either don't think like this at all, or they think like this only under extreme conditions (as was the case with Intel). This type of thinking should occur regularly. Our advice to teams is to ask these very specific types of self-evaluation questions at least once per quarter.

1. If we were looking at our company for the first time, what is the one thing we would recommend be improved?
2. If we were one of our clients, what is the one thing we would most like to see improved in terms of how we conduct business?
3. What is the one thing we most hope our opposition does not do?

WHEN TO MAKE ADJUSTMENTS

"Timing is everything" is a cliché for a reason.

It's true.

Adjustments are quicker to happen in sports than in many other types of organizations because time is limited. There is urgency for everyone involved. Coaches and players alike know that the "product" will be on the field every week for the world to view. If the team doesn't show high-level success in basic fundamentals, as well as necessary adjustments in the allotted game clock, the entire organization becomes accountable to the fans and the media. The consequences are immediate. Knowing this supplies ample motivation for making needed adjustments efficiently.

In business there is no game clock. And that means there's a false sense of security, because teams have a tendency to think, "It will be all right. We have time to fix this."

Plenty of otherwise talented leaders and managers fail not because they didn't understand that adjustments needed to happen—but because they didn't understand when the adjustments should have been initiated.

In virtually every case, it happens because leaders and teams don't make the proper adjustments in time, and they fall behind the curve.

This happens for two main reasons. The first reason is that when teams see success, they're extremely resistant to changing up a good thing. This works, so why should we change it?

But today's market isn't necessarily what tomorrow's will be. We're not suggesting that you blow things up just for the sake of doing it. But you can't ever stop evaluating where you are in relation to your customers and competitors and trying to see the future.

To see this in action, you don't have to look any further than the NFL. In that league, contracts aren't guaranteed from year to year. Players often sign three- and five-year contracts for big money, but in reality, the team is able to cut a player after any given year if the player doesn't produce. Each team's front office is ruthlessly evaluating every player—from the stars down to the last man on the roster—to make sure the salary figure they represent is a good representation of the value they provide on the field.

When that gets out of whack, teams will not hesitate to cut even the most beloved veteran stars. When general managers get too sentimental, their teams pay the price. That's why Peyton Manning didn't finish his career in Indianapolis. He was an icon, but his performance wasn't going to match his contract. Indianapolis moved on.

Medical technology has done incredible things for extending our life expectancy. But you still have to have a doctor who is paying attention to the small signals that something could be wrong. If somebody sees the signals, you have way more time to use modern medicine to your advantage.

Team members fill this same role. On a team operating at peak efficiency, the players have their fingers on the pulse of the market. They're able to deliver market, customer, and competitor information to leaders, where it gets examined for potential trends.

What does this mean for you as a team member or team leader? Your value is inextricably tied to your ability to recognize and evaluate base-level situations to assess whether your team needs to make an adjustment.

One of the most common laments we hear from our clients is about how they saw something that they sensed might become important, but they didn't react to it at the time—and with more time, it became a giant problem with no easy solutions.

Understand that very small adjustments can have a big impact if you make them early enough in the game. To have confidence making adjustments, you must know when they are necessary. Adjustments are needed when:

- The competition is improving faster than you are
- You are not in the lead
- There is an impending change in the market

Once you recognize that an adjustment is needed, there are three very important steps to follow.

Step 1: Decide on Your One Thing

Go back to one of the first things you've heard us say—about channel capacity. People can't make focused change on more than one thing at a time—and it just so happens that *adjusting* more than one variable at a time makes it incredibly hard to judge the effectiveness of any particular adjustment.

Never underestimate the big impact that one small adjustment might make.

When adjustments are needed, proceed with one adjustment at a time. Trying to make more than one improvement at a time, as previously stated, dishonors channel capacity and will usually result in flaws in the execution of the adjustment. Here are some guidelines for deciding on the most impactful adjustment you can make:

1. Always begin with the positive. Before making any adjustment, always evaluate, first, the two or three things your team is doing well. It is completely abnormal for teams to do this; however, skipping this step often leads to adjustments that are reactive and ineffective.
2. When you are already winning on the scoreboard, the questions is: What is one thing we *want* to improve?
3. When tied or losing on the scoreboard, the question is: What is one thing we *need* to improve?

Step 2: Attack, Attack, Attack

Whatever the adjustment, approach it with the attack mentality. Move on it aggressively and don't second-guess yourself. For effective adjustments to be made, people need to understand the "why" behind those adjustments. They need to make the mental adjustment before executing the strategic adjustment.

The marketing consultant Simon Sinek has pointed out that only teams that know their "why" can or will be inspired. In fact, the title of his 2009 book was *Start with Why: How Great Leaders Inspire Everyone to Take Action.* That title drives home the point that making adjustments efficiently and successfully requires individuals to believe in the "why." Executing adjustments requires inspiration and conviction.[3]

Explain the rationale for all adjustments to your people. Be clear on what the benefit is to the team, and more importantly, what the benefit is to them personally. Doing so will dramatically increase the probability of success.

The "why" is something that inspires. For General Patton, the "why" wasn't to win the war with as few American casualties as possible—that was the what. The "why" was to liberate good people from evil.

For Steve Jobs, the "why" wasn't to sell as many computers as possible. It was to buck the status quo and provide an elevated human experience.

For Mother Teresa, the "why" wasn't to open hospitals. It was to love people unconditionally.

And for John Wooden, the "why" wasn't to win games and national titles. It was to redefine success as the "peace of mind that results from the self-satisfaction that comes from knowing you made the effort to become the best you are capable of becoming."

In all four cases, mental and strategic adjustments combined to produce unbelievable outcomes.

Step 3: Evaluate

One way the world of science and the world of business are the same is how they treat results. Both have a long tradition of valuing concrete measurables. If you're a scientist and you can't produce measurable results in an experiment, you're still talking about a hypothesis—not fact.

When we're called in to work with an organization, leadership isn't looking for some squishy, abstract improvement in their teams' "feelings" or "attitudes." They're looking for measurable results. Improved sales figures. Better conversion. Higher batting averages. More victories.

There is an old saying in science: "If you can't measure it, it doesn't exist." With any adjustment, there must be a unit of measure that you will use to see if it led to improvement. If you cannot measure the effect of the change, it will be very difficult to make future decisions on further adjustments. **Most people think there must be some complex system for measuring impact and outcome, and that is just not true.** In fact, as with most things, the simpler the better.

This is yet another reason for adjusting only one thing at a time. It becomes profoundly more difficult to measure impact when more than one variable is being manipulated simultaneously.

Jason and Tom often follow a simple way of evaluating the success of an adjustment. Generally speaking, if the adjustment is being executed at 90 percent or better for thirty days, you should see about 70 percent of the impact. If the adjustment is executed 90 percent of the time for ninety days or longer, you should see at least 90 percent of the outcome the adjustment will produce.

We are not suggesting that you give all adjustments ninety days' time to make an impact, or that ninety days will be enough time to see the impact in all instances. Not at all. We aren't even saying that all adjustments need to be employed for thirty days. This is just a very simple way of evaluating adjustments that often, but not always, provides effective feedback.

The main point we are trying to make is that you need to have a way of measuring the outcome of adjustments, and the more simplified the method of evaluation, the more effective it will probably be. It was Albert Einstein who said that **there are five ascending levels of intelligence: smart, intelligent, brilliant, genius, and simple**.

We have found with high performers that it is also very important to learn to trust your instincts when it comes to making adjustments. If adjustments have been made and it doesn't seem like it is making the impact desired, then simply ask yourself this question: Is this making the change that I thought it would? Also ask this: If I were to look at this situation for the first time, what is the one adjustment I believe would make the greatest positive impact?

The most common trap when making adjustments is to not know when to readjust. Warren Buffet and Charlie Munger describe it as "loss aversion."[4] It boils down to people feeling like they have invested too much already to turn back or change course. Take, for example, the psychology of investing: it is very common for someone to purchase a stock with the hopes and promise of that stock providing huge returns.

Over time, though, if the stock severely underperforms, the investor feels compelled to keep the stock, still holding onto the false hope of it someday turning around, and not wanting to realize the loss. Nobody wants to look at the balance of the trade and see that they lost real dollars.

But the way the best investors approach every trade is to look at their position and continually ask themselves one question: If I had to buy this stock today at this price, would I feel like it was a good buy?

If buying the stock at that price is not the most intelligent investment today, then the stock should be sold, and the money should be put into a new, better investment.

This is exactly what they did at Intel, and it's exactly what you should do when evaluating your organization's current and future adjustments.

COMMON ADJUSTMENTS

We keep talking about adjustments, but what do these actually look like? In this section, we want to talk about some of the common issues we see with our clients and the concrete adjustments that have worked in those situations.

One of the most common issues comes from teams that see their raw scheduling fill up, but productivity doesn't increase. The team is busier than ever, but the work isn't translating into dollars. This is most often a result of channel capacity being violated. Team members are being stretched across different projects and different accounts, so they aren't able to service any of them the way they would normally. The answer is to have each team member reestablish and prioritize the "3 Most Important" and "1 Must" activities they need to attack each day.

When a previously high-achieving team starts to see a slowdown in new business, that's usually a result of not managing expectations correctly. It's especially common when teams have lots of business and are not able to accurately predict when they can deliver. New clients get frustrated because they're waiting around, and current accounts often get aggravated because, when they ask for adjustments, they get pushed to the back of the line. The solution is usually to create scripts of "what clients should expect from our team" for team members to use with clients and prospects that more accurately manage expectations of service, costs, and project timelines.

If your team seems to be stagnating or not growing as fast as the competition, identify for each person on the team the "1 Must" activity that needs to be completed daily. Then do whatever it takes to have each person "attack" his or her one thing first thing every day.

Politics and personalities are a part of any group of human beings. Teams obviously aren't immune to politics. What happens when you have to deal with infighting among the members of the team? You're not going to be able to wave a wand and make them all act like friends. But you can create a culture of acknowledgment and appreciation. Ask each team member at the end of the day to identify a teammate who has done something well ("point")—something that contributes to the overall success of the team. This can be done in a public forum, such as a "done-well board" that everyone sees, or in a group email, or even by ending the day with a brief team huddle.

If you sense that the team is taking on a victim mentality, make the adjustment of helping people recognize that it is happening. Remind people that in every negative situation, there is *always* something that can be done to improve. Make the rule that people are not allowed to focus on the negative or the problem, but rather must focus on, talk about, and take action toward the one solution.

When teammates are disagreeable, adjust by beginning all conversations with this statement: "The one thing I appreciate most about your opinion is . . ." The goal then becomes combining positive points from differing opinions to create a stronger approach.

TEACH IT

Making adjustments is difficult and will often take great courage. Tom Bartow said something many years ago that is as true today as it was when he first said it: "If you let fear for self come before helping others, you will surely fail."

INVERT

(By inverting any fundamental you can learn more)

When a team doesn't make adjustments, it no longer becomes a question of whether they will fail, but when they will fail. If you don't believe us, just look at former companies like Blockbuster, Kodak, and Borders Books.

"3 MOST IMPORTANT" FOR THE TEAM TO REMEMBER

1. There are "strategic" adjustments and there are "mental" adjustments. Strategic adjustments are changes in the approach, process, or method of conducting business. Mental adjustments are changes in attitude or perspective.

2. Mental adjustments are simple in nature but seldom tried in business. A mental adjustment is made when an individual comes to understand the benefit, the purpose, or the rationale of the strategic adjustment. Mental adjustments are more important than strategic adjustments because they serve as the fuel and conviction for the execution of the strategic adjustments as well as for follow-through.

3. There are three very important steps when making adjustments:

    a. **Decide on Your "One Thing"**: Never underestimate the big impact that one small adjustment can make.

    b. **Attack, Attack, Attack:** Be certain everyone knows the purpose of the adjustment and its personal and organizational benefits. Knowing the "why" will significantly increase conviction among team members to execute the adjustment.

    c. **Evaluate:** Settle on a unit of measure and period of time so you can track the adjustment and determine whether it is producing the desired outcomes. If not, readjust.

continues

continued

"1 MUST" TAKEAWAY FOR TEAMS

It's a fact of life that most organizations don't make mental adjustments. This is why very few of them reach the dynasty level. Always find the mental adjustments needed to create conviction and "buy-in" for strategic adjustments among team members.

EPILOGUE

S o what now?

You've gotten to the end of the book. We hope you're filled with great ideas to take back to your team—whether it's one you're a part of on the front lines, or one you're leading.

As we have consistently stated throughout the book, it's not what you know that will change your life, but rather, what you *do* with what you know. That's what will make the difference.

If you want to move your team from winning consistently to becoming a dynasty, please take the following three steps. These three steps will speed up the process.

1. RESIST—Respect channel capacity and resist the temptation to try everything at once. The single biggest mistake we see from the people we coach is that they try to make more than one improvement at a time.
2. CHOOSE ONE—The most effective method of using this book and taking your game to the next level is to choose one chapter for you and/or your team to implement. Until you have nailed one concept (90 percent of the time for a minimum of thirty days), resist the temptation to attack another.
3. "ATTACK, ALWAYS ATTACK"—No matter which one chapter you choose, always attack! Set a time period every day (even if for just five minutes) when you will be

completely focused and get all over the one thing you have set your sights on. This is where the real progress and growth occur.

By trusting the process, you will *speed up* the process. It happens for our clients every week, both in the business world and in the world of sports. It happens for elite athletes and Fortune 500 CEOs just like it happens for the average person sharing an office in a town that looks just like yours.

You'll be ready to become your own dynasty.

Notes

CHAPTER 2

1. Stephen R. Covey, *The Seven Habits of Highly Effective People: Powerful Lessons in Personal Change*, 25th Anniversary Edition (New York: Simon and Schuster, 2013).

2. Major Robert J. Rielly, "Confronting the Tiger: Small Unit Cohesion in Battle," *Military Review*, November/December 2000.

CHAPTER 3

1. Og Mandino, *The Greatest Secret in the World* (New York: Bantam Books, 2009).

2. Carol S. Dweck, *Mindset: The New Psychology of Success* (New York: Random House, 2006).

CHAPTER 4

1. Steven Covey, *The 8th Habit: From Effectiveness to Greatness* (New York: Free Press, 2004).

2. Peter Bevelin, *Seeking Wisdom: From Darwin to Munger*, 3rd ed. (Lawrenceville, GA: PCA Publications, 2007).

CHAPTER 5

1. Porter B. Williamson, *General Patton's Principles for Life and Leadership*, 5th ed. (Tucson, AZ: Management and Systems Consultants, 2009).

2. Dale Carnegie, *How to Win Friends and Influence People* (New York: Simon and Schuster, 2009), 135–136.

3. Chris Ballard, "No Coach, No Problem," *Sports Illustrated*, May 29, 2017, https://www.si.com/vault/2017/05/23/no-coach-no -problem.

4. Stephen R. Covey, *The Seven Habits of Highly Effective People: Powerful Lessons in Personal Change*, 25th Anniversary Edition (New York: Simon and Schuster, 2013).

CHAPTER 6

1. Urban Meyer, *Above the Line: Lessons in Leadership and Life from a Champion Season* (New York: Penguin, 2015).

2. Col. Edward L. Hubbard, *Escape from the Box: The Wonder of Human Potential* (West Chester, PA: Praxis, 1994).

3. Viktor Frankl, *Man's Search for Meaning* (Boston: Beacon Press, 2006 [1946]).

4. Gerry Spence, *How to Argue and Win Every Time: At Home, at Work, in Court, Everywhere, Every Day* (New York: St. Martin's, 1995).

CHAPTER 7

1. Carol S. Dweck, *Mindset: The New Psychology of Success* (New York: Random House, 2006).

2. James Morehead, "Stanford University's Carol Dweck on the Growth Mindset and Education," OneDublin.org, June 19, 2012,

https://onedublin.org/2012/06/19/stanford-universitys-carol-dweck -on-the-growth-mindset-and-education.

3. Sam Walton, *Made in America* (New York: Doubleday, 1992).

CHAPTER 9

1. Andrew S. Grove, *Only the Paranoid Survive* (New York: Doubleday, 1996).

2. Col. Edward L. Hubbard, *Escape from the Box: The Wonder of Human Potential* (West Chester, PA: Praxis, 1994).

3. Simon Sinek, *Start with Why: How Great Leaders Inspire Everyone to Take Action* (New York: Portfolio, 2009).

4. Peter Bevelin, *Seeking Wisdom: From Darwin to Munger*, 3rd ed. (Lawrenceville, GA: PCA Publications, 2007).

About the Authors

Dr. Jason Selk is one of the premier performance coaches in the United States. His clients include Olympians and professional athletes in Major League Baseball, the NFL, the NBA, the NHL, and NASCAR, along with Fortune 500 executives and organizations such as Northwestern Mutual and Edward Jones. As the director of mental training for Major League Baseball's St. Louis Cardinals, Dr. Selk helped the team win two World Series championships, in 2006 and 2011. He has previously written three best-selling books, *Organize Tomorrow Today* (coauthored with Tom Bartow, with Matthew Rudy), *10-Minute Toughness*, and *Executive Toughness*. He is a regular contributor to ESPN, *Inc.*, and *Forbes* and has been featured in *USA Today*, *Men's Health*, *Muscle & Fitness*, and *Self.* He lives outside of St. Louis, Missouri. You can find him at JasonSelk.com.

Tom Bartow left a successful career as a college baseball coach to become one of the top financial advisors at Edward Jones. As a partner, he applied many of the concepts he had learned from John Wooden, the famed basketball coach at UCLA, to create and develop an advanced training program for high-level advisors at the firm. In June 1999, the American Funds Group offered

Tom a unique position: one of his responsibilities was to work with American Funds distributors across the nation to increase the skillset of the entire sales organization. Tom's insights immediately proved to be highly beneficial to investors and advisors. From 2002 to 2009, Coach Wooden and Tom delivered a one-two punch for the American Funds Advisors Forums. Their friendship was such that Tom was invited to join Coach Wooden at the White House for Coach Wooden's acceptance of the Medal of Freedom. Coach Wooden said of Tom, "You are something else."

Tom Bartow and Dr. Jason Selk have become the best of friends and have worked together to bring peak performance techniques from the world of professional athletic competition to the corporate world.

Matthew Rudy has authored or coauthored twenty-three golf, business, and travel books, including titles with Hank Haney, Dr. Michael Lardon, Dave Stockton, and Johnny Miller. He is a senior writer at *Golf Digest*, where he has produced more than twenty-five cover stories since 1999. He lives in Bridgeport, Connecticut. You can find him at MatthewRudy.net, or on Twitter at @RudyWriter.

Index

disagreements *(continued)*
  arguments different from, 107
  between boss and employee, 107
  creating spirit of agreeable
    disagreement, 108–109
  encouraging, 98
  fear and suspicion and, 105–107
  ground rules for, 109–110
  hierarchy of relationships, 105
  interruptions, 109, 118
  open-mindedness, 104
  phrases/terms to open the lines
    of communication, 101–102
  questions to ask concerning,
    100, 108
  within teams, 72, 113, 199
  understanding value of, 110
distraction, 85, 88–89
done-well board, 199
Duncan, Dave, 32, 51–52
Durant, Kevin, 103
Dweck, Carol, 54, 145
dynasty, vii, ix–xii, 24
  adjustments and, 181, 187, 202
  response to adversity, 119–120
  steps to becoming, 203–204

Eastern Illinois University, 122,
  124
Edward Jones, viii, 4, 11–12, 130,
  134, 151–152
8th Habit, The, 73
Einstein, Albert, 197
Emotional Intelligence (Goleman),
  145
endorsement, 45, 105
energy decreased by stress, 188
Escape from the Box (Hubbard),
  125, 187

evaluation. *See also* self-evaluation
  art of, 59–61
  performance, 62–63, 65
  when to evaluate, 62–63
excuses
  refusing to use, 42–43, 47, 50,
    106, 120, 168
  underachieving promoted by,
    129
execution, inconsistent/poor, 7,
  18
exercise, 164–165
expectancy theory, 58, 129
expectations. *See also* managing
    expectations
  delivering on, 28
  mismanaging, 28, 41
  setting, 28
eye-closing while listening,
  115–116

Facebook, 97, 99
failure, 145
fear, 125
  disagreements and, 105
  in hierarchy of relationships, 38,
    49, 105
  leadership based on, 105–107
  for self, 200
  of speaking up, 110
feedback, 156, 196
fiduciary responsibility, 135
fighting-through, 167–169, 174
financial advisors
  developing, 150–152
  process goals, 155
first problem, 10
fixed-mindset, 54, 145
flexibility, 181. *See also* adjustments